Praise for *How to Stop Losing Your Sh*t with Your Kids*

'*How to Stop Losing Your Sh*t with Your Kids* will make you laugh out loud, nod in agreement, and cry tears of relief as you realize that you are not alone and you do have the power to make healthy changes that benefit the whole family. Highly recommended during any stage of the parenting journey.'
Katie Hurley, LCSW, author of *No More Mean Girls*
and *The Happy Kid Handbook*

'Funny, honest and real, this is the book I needed when my kids were toddlers – and middle graders – and yesterday afternoon. Naumburg reminds me that I have to deal with my own shit to have a fighting chance at helping my kids deal with theirs, and she doesn't shy away from hard truths and challenges about the process, or skimp on practical ideas for getting there. I'm going to need multiple copies of this one – one for me, and one for pretty much everyone else I know.'
KJ Dell'Antonia, author of *How to Be a Happier Parent: Raising a Family, Having a Life and Loving (Almost) Every Minute*

'Reading this book is like going to the best parenting class and leaving feeling taken care of and motivated to make changes. Naumburg's concrete tips, honesty, and thought-provoking suggestions will inspire and empower you.'
Catherine Pearlman, PhD, LCSW, author of *Ignore It! How Selectively Looking the Other Way Can Decrease Behavioral Problems and Increase Parenting Satisfaction*

'Makes you feel hugged rather than judged. By the end not only are you laughing your ass off, but you've gained a sense of self-compassion and a concrete action plan. Part self-help manual, part funny textbook (complete with helpful metaphors and saucy acronyms), and part poignant memoir, *How to Stop Losing Your Sh*t with Your Kids* is a must-read for any parent!'
Rebecca Schrag Hershberg, PhD,
author of *The Tantrum Survival Guide*

'This book hits the trifecta: it's enjoyable, easy to read, and full of expert information I will actually use. It's like sitting down with a really wise, funny friend who has all the answers, but doesn't act like she does. It's already in my top five parenting books you have to read!'

Kate Rope, author of *Strong as a Mother: How to Stay Happy, Healthy, and (Most Importantly) Sane from Pregnancy to Parenthood*

'This wise, compassionate book will give comfort and useful ideas to every parent, whether they lose their sh*t once a year – or once a day!'

Katherine Reynolds Lewis, author of *The Good News About Bad Behavior*

HOW TO STOP LOSING YOUR SH*T WITH YOUR KIDS

Effective strategies for stressed-out parents

CARLA NAUMBURG, PHD

First published in Great Britain in 2019 by Yellow Kite
An imprint of Hodder & Stoughton
An Hachette UK company

First published in the United States in 2019
by Workman Publishing Company, Inc.

This paperback edition published in 2020

8

A CIP catalogue record for this title is available from the British Library

Paperback ISBN 978 1 529 32973 5
eBook ISBN 978 1 473 68695 3

Printed and bound in Great Britain by Clays Ltd, Elcograf S.p.A.

Hodder & Stoughton policy is to use papers that are natural, renewable
and recyclable products and made from wood grown in sustainable forests.
The logging and manufacturing processes are expected to conform to the
environmental regulations of the country of origin.

Yellow Kite
Hodder & Stoughton Ltd
Carmelite House
50 Victoria Embankment
London EC4Y 0DZ

www.yellowkitebooks.co.uk

. . . .

For my daughters,
without whom I never would have
lost my shit in the first place

. . . .

For my husband,
who rarely loses his shit
and still loves me
no matter how often I lose mine

. . . .

Acknowledgments

This book wouldn't be possible without the help and guidance of Gillian MacKenzie, agent extraordinaire, and Margot Herrera and her fantastic team at Workman, including Rebecca Carlisle, Page Edmunds, Lisa Hollander, Moira Kerrigan, Beth Levy, Lathea Mondesir, and Elissa Santos. In addition, I am eternally grateful to the teachers at my daughters' school for teaching them all day so I could write.

This book is so much stronger thanks to the honest, wise, and hilarious feedback from friends and my advance readers: Rachel Barbanel-Fried, Mayim Bialik, Dave Cutler, Kathleen Flinton, Alex McAdam, and Kate Rope.

Thank you to the fabulous book coach, Lisa Tener, who helped me craft my book proposal, and to my therapist, Heather, who saved my butt six ways to Saturday every Tuesday afternoon. I wouldn't have made it through the long writing days without my social media crew, who answered my random questions about '90s TV shows and caffeine drinks. I also want to thank my cats, who don't give a crap about this book but kept me company nonetheless.

I am so lucky to have the most amazing support system. So much love to my amazing sister, Daniela Silverstein, who has been with me through everything, and to my many dear friends, including Mara Acel-Green, Rachel Fish, Rachel Pytel, and Ali Wolf.

Last but not least, thank you to my husband and daughters, for, well, everything. You are my everything.

CONTENTS

It's Time to Stop Losing Your Shit

THE TRUTH ABOUT PARENTAL SHIT LOSS

★

IT'S NOT YOUR FAULT

★

YOU *CAN* GET IT TOGETHER

So, you're losing your shit with your kids. You snap, shout, and scream at them. You're irritable and reactive more often than you'd like to admit. You know how you want to parent; you want to be calmer and more intentional. But no matter how hard you try, you keep losing it.

Without knowing anything else about you or your family or your particular style of freak-out, I can tell you six truths that will help you feel less ashamed and more empowered to deal with your shit instead of losing it.

Six Truths About Parental Shit Loss

1. PARENTING IS HARD. It's hard for everyone. No, really, everyone—even that Seemingly Perfect Parent, always in the front of the pickup line with her skinny soy latte and carefully vacuumed minivan. Parenting is hard for a lot of different reasons, some of which have to do with you, some of which have to do with your kid, and some of which seem more closely aligned with the phases of the moon than anything down here on planet Earth.

2. EVERY PARENT LOSES THEIR SHIT SOMETIMES. Some lose it more often, more loudly, or more publicly than others, but we all lose it. You are absolutely, positively, without a single doubt not alone in this. The *New York Times* published an article a few years ago that described shouting as the new spanking and labeled us "a generation that yells."

3. CONTRARY TO WHAT YOU MAY THINK, YOU PROBABLY HAVEN'T BROKEN YOUR CHILDREN. Don't get me wrong; your meltdowns are not good for them or you or anybody. But you already know that. What you may not know is that humans are more resilient than we give ourselves credit for; many of us were raised by shit-losers and have grown up to be functional, productive members of society with only mild to moderate Ben & Jerry addictions. This means you can let go of some of the guilt, stress, and shame you've been hanging on to, and you probably don't need to fully fund the kids' therapy accounts just yet.

4. EVEN SO, LOSING YOUR SHIT SUCKS. It's exhausting and feels awful for everyone. It stresses out your kids, strains your relationship with them, and makes you doubt yourself and your parenting abilities. Your meltdowns use up precious time and energy without actually fixing the problem or preventing it from happening again, and they make it harder for you to be the kind of parent you want to be. To top it all off, you're also modeling the very behavior you don't want to see in your kids.

5. IT'S NOT A MATTER OF WILLPOWER. Many parents assume they should be able to just decide not to lose their shit and then have the inner strength to grit their teeth and get through difficult moments without exploding. While some of us can do that some of the time, willpower isn't as predictable or reliable as we'd like to think it is. So, if you feel like you're not strong enough to hold it together, remember: It's not about strength or willpower. It's about understanding what causes meltdowns, and having the skills and strategies to deal with them effectively.

6. YOU CAN LEARN HOW TO LOSE YOUR SHIT A WHOLE LOT LESS OFTEN and how to recover more quickly when you do lose it. This isn't going to happen overnight, and it will take some work on your part, but as they say, the best things in life aren't free and your kids will probably break them anyway, so we're not going for the best. We're just going for better than what we have now.

Now is probably a pretty good time to mention that if you're looking for a 100 percent Money-Back Guarantee that you will never ever lose your shit again after reading this book, well, that ain't gonna happen. The good news for you and me and the rest of us imperfect parents trying to raise slightly less imperfect children is that you don't have to be the Dalai Mama in order to be more intentional and less insane with your kids. That having been said, every time you manage to stay calm instead of freaking out, you create space to respond thoughtfully and parent the way you want to—however that looks for you and your family.

Fortunately, you can do this without turning your life upside down or hiring a Super Nanny or investing in some stupidly expensive twenty-seven-step program that will completely overwhelm you before you even get to Step Three. Using simple instructions, I'll show you what you need to do to stop losing your temper. The habits and practices I recommend in this book will not just help you be a chiller, more patient parent, they will also help you be generally happier, more productive, and more in control of every other aspect of your life.

This may not be the first thing you've read on how to stop yelling or how to stay calm when your buttons are being pushed, and I'm guessing that the other advice hasn't worked—otherwise you wouldn't be here. I get it. I've read all of the articles and top-ten lists too, and not just because I had to as part of my research for this book. I first sought them out one particularly awful evening a few years ago when I plunked my tiny tyrants down in front of Daniel Tiger so I could have approximately twenty-two minutes to google "how to stop yelling at my kids." Bear in mind I have a PhD in clinical social work, and I was reduced to googling that shit. If you're confused about how to deal with all of this, you're definitely not alone.

Why You Haven't Gotten Your Shit Together Yet
(SPOILER ALERT: IT'S NOT YOUR FAULT)

In my personal and professional experience, there are a few different reasons why much of the advice out there doesn't work for most parents.

> **You don't need to be a perfect parent to be a great parent.**

★ Many of those books are just too damn long, and most parents don't have the time, energy, or desire to read all those words. I promise to get to the point.

★ The advice holds parents and children to unrealistic standards and practices that may be great in theory but are impossible to execute in real life. When the suggestions you're reading don't pan out, you end up feeling like a failure, and you give up. I'm a working parent (my daughters are eight and ten years old), and I'm not going to dish out anything I wouldn't serve up in my own house. This is also a good time to remind you yet again that you don't need to be a perfect parent to be a great parent. The more you stress about perfection, the more likely you are to lose your shit, which is super ironic, but not in a cool hipster kind of way.

★ Most advice focuses on the moment of the freak-out, often by telling you what you should do instead of losing it. I like to think of these as "shoulda coulda woulda" suggestions. You know you should do ten jumping jacks or take fourteen deep breaths instead of yelling, and if you coulda done that, you woulda done that, so clearly you need a different approach. I've got one.

★ The advice wasn't the right match for you or your family. Exhibit A: I once read a suggestion that I should yell into the toilet instead of yelling at my kids. While this strategy probably worked for the parent who wrote it, I had one kid in diapers and one in the throes of potty-training hell. The last thing I wanted to do was spend more time around poop receptacles. The advice in this book is universal and easy to tweak to fit your preferences and style.

★ Finally, there is very little advice about what to do *after* the inevitable freak-out happens (which it will, no matter what). The reality is that there are better and worse ways to respond to yourself and your children after you lose your shit. The more effective strategies will help you recover more quickly and make it less likely that you'll explode again any time soon, so we're gonna go ahead and focus on those.

The point here is that if you haven't yet been able to stop losing it, it's not because you're a failure. And it's certainly not because there is anything wrong with you, either as a person or a parent. This is a really important point so I'm going to repeat it again in capital letters: YOU ARE NOT A BAD PARENT. Parenting is hard, losing your shit is

WHY THERE'S NO SUCH THING AS A BAD PARENT

SOME OF YOU may be thinking that there are actually bad parents out there, mothers and fathers who behave terribly, who hit their children, or threaten, shame, and neglect them on a regular basis. Maybe you even think you're one of them. Maybe you're right, maybe you're not, but either way, I still refuse to call anyone a "bad parent." It's just not helpful. Once you've been stuck with a label like that, there's nowhere to go, no path toward change and healing. Rather than talking about bad parents, let's talk about parents who are struggling—a lot—and don't yet have the right information, resources, and support. From that place of compassion, we can think about where to go next.

part of the universal human condition, and you just haven't gotten the right mix of advice and support yet. You can do this. I promise.

STEP 1: UNDERSTAND WHY YOU'RE LOSING YOUR SHIT

First off, we need to get clear on what it means to lose your shit and why you keep doing it. The short story is that your buttons are being pushed. The longer story is about why you have so many buttons, how parenting makes them so damn sensitive, and what exactly happens when they're pushed.

Making sense of this process requires us to step inside your mind and body for a minute. Once you understand what triggers your nervous system and how those triggers lead to your loss of shit, you'll realize that it's not about some moral failing or innate weakness on your part. It's about normal human wiring, which propels a Fight, Flight, Freeze, or Freak Out reaction when your buttons are pushed, even if such a response is decidedly unhelpful. Fortunately, when you understand not only what's happening but also why it happens, you'll feel less out of control and ashamed, and more empowered and equipped to work *with* your nutso brain rather than being flattened by it every time it gets overwhelmed.

STEP 2: OWN YOUR BUTTONS AND YOUR TRIGGERS

We're going to start by talking about your buttons and triggers. For the purposes of this book, your "buttons" are your nervous system and a "trigger" is anything that revs up your nervous system and makes your buttons bigger, brighter, more sensitive, and way easier for your kids to push. And your children *will* push your buttons. They are genetically, evolutionarily, physiologically, developmentally, relationally, psychologically, and emotionally wired to jam their sticky little fingers into your buttons every chance they get. Some kids push harder and faster than other kids, but they all push. It doesn't mean they secretly despise you. It just means they're your kids.

Many parenting books focus on how to get kids to stop with all the pushing already. While it is technically your job as a parent to teach your children to keep their hands to themselves, both literally and figuratively, this is not the best tactic for managing your shit. Do you really want to hinge your sanity on the behavior of someone who licks walls and melts down over the shape of a piece of toast? Yeah, I didn't think so.

> A "trigger" is anything that revs up your nervous system and makes your buttons bigger, brighter, more sensitive, and way easier for your kids to push.

Fortunately, there's a better plan. You're going to get to know your buttons. You're going to learn what lights them up (aka your triggers) and how to cool them down. The good news is this stuff is pretty simple and straightforward, and it will be helpful in every area of your life, not just parenting. The bad news is that it ain't always easy, especially for busy parents who may be triggered most of the time. The other good news is that you're a parent, which means you can do hard things.

STEP 3: GET YOUR SHIT TOGETHER

For some parents, a little insight into how buttons and triggers can lead to parental shit loss is enough to lead to significant change. Once you can clearly see the ways that certain situations or experiences activate your nervous system, you suddenly feel a lot less triggered. That's great when it happens, but most folks need more than just insight. Most folks also need to learn how, exactly, to make their buttons as small and dim and pushproof as possible. This is commonly referred to as self-care, which makes lots of parents all twitchy, so, for the purposes of this book, let's

WHY KIDS PUSH BUTTONS

KIDS PUSH BUTTONS for lots of different reasons. They do it because they want our attention, they're trying to get what they need, and they don't have the maturity or impulse control to do otherwise. Sometimes they're just doing what kids do, and what kids do can be loud and stinky and annoying. In addition, children will be more likely to push buttons when they're triggered—because they're tired, hungry, confused, scared, excited, anxious, or otherwise overwhelmed by Big Feelings. It is totally reasonable to help your children in these moments, to redirect, feed, or soothe them. Each time you do that, you're modeling an effective way to respond to their triggers. Just remember, it is not your job to get them to stop pushing. Your job is to teach them, again and again, to notice and respond skillfully to their triggers (which, for the record, is exactly what this book will teach you to do as well) and to take care of your own buttons so they'll be much harder to push.

think of it as Shit You Have to Do If You Don't Want to Lose Your Shit. Fortunately, it's not super complicated and you don't have to do it perfectly all the time. You're not training for a marathon. You're just trying to have a little more patience the next time that munchkin asks for a snack twenty minutes after she refused to eat her dinner.

STEP 4: **DON'T LOSE YOUR SHIT**

The more you can get your shit together (by managing your buttons and reducing your triggers), the less likely you will be to lose it with your kids.

But (because there's always a *but*), there will be buttons left to push. You know it and I know it and, worst of all, your kids know it too. They know it better than they know their own tablets. The moment they stop tapping on those damn screens, they'll start tap-tap-tapping away at you. When that happens, you have two choices: You can either lose it or do Literally Anything Else.

I'm guessing you're interested in what's behind Door Number Two—otherwise you picked up the wrong book. The secret to staying calm is self-awareness; it's about *noticing* you're about to explode and giving yourself a chance to calm down. Noticing is your Power Play; it's what makes all those "shoulda coulda woulda" suggestions possible. The ability to realize that your shoulders are getting tight and your chest is getting hot (and for the love of God will the damn kid just get her shoes on already) is the key to not freaking out. If you never notice you're on the verge, you can't choose to take a few steps back and calm down instead.

The minute you become aware that you're in, or about to be in, Full-On Freak-Out Mode, you can pause and go into Literally Any Other Mode. The key to this is remembering that (a) noticing is a skill, which means you can get better at it, and (b) you can notice, pause, and change direction at any moment—even as the angry tirade is erupting from your mouth—without undermining your own authority or losing the battle or looking like an idiot in front of your kids or whatever else it is that you're worried about.

> **If you never notice you're on the verge, you can't choose to take a few steps back and calm down instead.**

No, really, you can. I'll show you how, and with some practice (don't worry, your kids will give you lots of opportunities to practice), you will get better at it.

STEP 5: AFTER THE SHITSTORM HAS PASSED

I said you'll get better at it. I never said you'll be perfect. (Now is probably a good time to introduce you to your new mantra: *Perfection can suck it.*) You will still lose it sometimes. While it can be tempting to pretend like nothing happened, I don't recommend it. Leaving things hanging is confusing for you and your child, and can make it even more likely that you'll lose it again.

Fortunately, there are choices you can make after the meltdown that will get you into a better headspace, help you repair your relationship with your kiddo, and keep you calm the next time your buttons are pushed. There are two good ways to do this, and the sooner you can get your head into either one, the faster that storm cloud hanging out right above you will float on by.

You can either have a little compassion for yourself or get curious about what happened. Those are your ideal options. I mean, another choice is to beat yourself up, perhaps by mentally ticking off all the different ways you suck at parenting and how you're permanently traumatizing your child. You could even throw in a few unhelpful comparisons; if you can't come up with anyone on your own, social media will do the trick in an instant. Unfortunately, there are a couple of problems with sending yourself down yet another shame spiral: (1) it feels terrible, and (2) it actually makes it more likely that you'll lose it again, which is the opposite of what you're trying to accomplish. Self-compassion isn't just useful for recovering from meltdowns; it's also an excellent strategy for preventing them in the first place. We'll explore compassion more in Chapter 5. In Chapter 9, we'll dive into how compassion and curiosity can shift your perspective and mood quickly and effectively, as well as how to integrate them into your post-meltdown recovery.

> There are choices you can make after the meltdown that will get you into a better headspace, help you repair your relationship with your kiddo, and keep you calm the next time your buttons are pushed.

Hopefully by now you've got a sense of how this book can help you. You may be tempted to head straight to Chapter 8 (What You've Been Waiting For: How, Exactly, to Not Lose Your Shit) and skip all the stuff about your buttons and triggers, but please don't do that. Trying to stay calm when you haven't slept in three days and your mother won't stop calling and you're freaking out about how you're going to cover your rent this month is impossible. But once you get a little clarity on what you're facing and start dealing with it, you'll be more likely to stay calm in tough moments. In addition, once you know how to notice that you're about to fall off Freak-Out Cliff, you'll be able to stop yourself in time, or at least cushion your landing.

Most importantly, remember that you're not alone. This is hard for everyone, and you can do it. I'm here to help.

CHAPTER 1

Why Are You Losing Your Shit?

COMMON FEATURES OF
PARENTAL FREAK-OUTS

★

THE DOWNSIDES OF
EXPLODING

★

WHY IT'S SO HARD TO
STOP LOSING YOUR SHIT

★

A WEE BIT OF
BRAIN SCIENCE

First up, we need to get clear on what I mean by losing your shit. Grown-up meltdowns look a little different for each of us. They're a bit like pornography in that way. No, not like that. Geez. I mean that they can be hard to define, but we know them when we see them.

How to Know If You Are Losing Your Shit

Most episodes of shit loss share a few common character-istics, which we can remember with the acronym **FART** (**F**eelings, **A**utomatic, **R**eactive, **T**oxic). Not the sexiest acronym, but hopefully it will remind you that you're not alone. Like flatulence, losing your temper is an unfortunate yet completely normal part of the human condition. Everyone does it (even though some of us try to pretend we don't). While we can make changes in our life that may reduce our flatulence, it's still going to happen. The good news is, if we notice it's coming, we can take steps to mitigate the impact. Also, and most importantly, I will take every opportunity I can to remind you that this parenting gig is far too serious to be taken seriously. So, yeah, we're gonna talk about FARTs.

Without further ado, here are the common features of most Parental Freak-Outs:

FEELINGS. Meltdowns generally involve Big Feelings, and not just anger or rage. Almost any strong emotion will do, including fear, sadness, confusion, power-

> We can't force ourselves to feel a particular way; all we can do is notice that we're actually having a feeling so we can choose how to respond.

lessness, stress, annoyance, anxiety, embarrassment, guilt, or shame. Even positive emotions can trigger us, as any parent who has seen a child laugh herself into tears knows. Sometimes our Big Feelings are related to our kids' antics, and sometimes they're not. Sometimes we're aware that we're having all the feelings, and sometimes we're not. What you need to remember is that (a) losing your shit is an emotional reaction, not a rational one, and (b) we don't have nearly as much control over our feelings as we'd like to think. We can't force ourselves to feel a particular way; all we can do is notice that we're actually having a feeling so we can choose how to respond.

AUTOMATIC. It's important to remember that most meltdowns are neither conscious nor intentional. It's not as though you come home from a bad day at work and think to yourself, "Huh. I'm pretty stressed. I think I'll go ahead and totally lose it on my kids tonight." In most cases, melting down is an unconscious process beyond your control, one that can often be traced back to your childhood and the ways your parents lost their tempers with you. This is why you can't simply decide to not lose your shit and then just not lose it. Your explosions are a predictable outcome of developmental, neurological, and biological processes, rather than logical decisions.

REACTIVE. We can think about reactivity in two ways. First, it's about what we say and do *in reaction* to something else. Something has to happen to get us to freak out; it doesn't come out of nowhere. Sometimes the reason for our freak-out is abundantly clear; we can draw a straight line from the trigger to the meltdown. Other times we have no clue why we lost it. Something may have happened five minutes, five hours, or five years ago, and it may have nothing to do with our kids. Whatever it is, and whenever it happened, identifying the thing you are reacting to is crucial. If you never realize that May is a terrible month for you because it's the anniversary of your first miscarriage, you can't make the choice to take extra care of yourself during that time. If you don't acknowledge that the pain in your molar isn't going to magically disappear, you can't suck it up and go to the dentist.

The other definition of reactivity has to do with our ability to act quickly *in response to real or perceived danger*. The human brain and body developed to keep us safe from physical threats. Unfortunately, they still haven't figured out that most of the stressors we face these days are emotional or psychological, and not life-threatening, so they react quickly to situations that don't require such intense and fast reactions. In addition, our brains aren't always great at telling the difference between Serious Problems and Minor Issues, which is why we end up with a shit-loss-level reaction even when it's not necessary.

TOXIC. Remember the last time your child darted into the street or nearly fell down the stairs? You probably had some Big Feelings that propelled you to react automatically, perhaps by yelling or quickly grabbing your child's arm. Even if you yelled or grabbed a bit harder than you intended to, I wouldn't categorize that as losing your shit. This is an example of your nervous system reacting appropriately in a potentially dangerous situation. The moment wasn't toxic, by which I mean unnecessarily harsh or harmful to your relationship with your kiddo. So, yes, it is possible to go FAR without FARTing.

THE MOST TOXIC EXPLOSIONS AND WHAT TO DO ABOUT THEM

ALTHOUGH THERE ARE many ways to lose your shit with your kids, some are worse than others. Insults and threats are particularly damaging, as is physical aggression or violence of any kind, including hitting, slapping, spanking, or throwing things. Perhaps this is part of the culture you were raised in or are parenting in, or maybe it's a new experience for you. Either way, if any of this is happening in your home, **it needs to stop**. First, do what you can to stop blaming and shaming yourself. Yes, the situation is serious, but the sooner you can find a little forgiveness and kindness for yourself, the sooner you'll be able to get some help and make some important changes. You're not the only parent to ever hit your child, but that doesn't mean it's OK. You can do better. I promise. You may not be able to do it alone, and that doesn't mean you've failed at parenting. It just means you're in over your head. Talking to someone you trust is the first step: It can be a friend or family member, your doctor or pediatrician, a therapist, counselor, minister, rabbi, priest, or imam. It's not going to be an easy conversation or an enjoyable one, but it needs to happen. You can do this.

Toxic explosions are unpredictable, disproportionate reactions that can include angry words, physical outbursts, personal attacks, shame, and blame. The moment feels out of control. Toxic outbursts happen when we are triggered, and they continue to trigger everyone involved. Examples may include screaming at your child over spilled cereal, exploding because he's taking too long to put on his shoes, or angrily berating a daughter for forgetting her homework. These reactive explosions can rupture and weaken the connection between you and your child.

In addition, frequent tension and stress mess with the brain and nervous systems, increasing the likelihood you'll be triggered in the future. This is why it's so important for you to figure out not only how to lose your shit less often, but also how to reconnect with your child each time it happens.

Just to recap: Losing our shit is about FARTing. There are Big **F**eelings involved, and our behavior is **A**utomatic, **R**eactive, and **T**oxic. Speaking of our behavior, there's a reason I didn't get all hung up on whether you snapped, screamed, or slammed, or just stalked off in a huff while muttering sarcastically under your breath. We all explode differently, with varying levels of intensity, so it's more helpful to focus on the characteristics rather than the actual behavior. I've seen silent stares that are just as hurtful as flying remote controls; I've heard steely threats that could rival Clint Eastwood on a bad day.

> Toxic explosions are unpredictable, disproportionate reactions that can include angry words, physical outbursts, personal attacks, shame, and blame.

Having said that, most of us resort to a few habitual behaviors (snapping, screaming, slamming, etc.) when we lose it, and it's super important that you get clear on exactly what you do when you freak out because that behavior is the *only* thing you can control.

> I've seen silent stares that are just as hurtful as flying remote controls.

I hope I just threw you for a loop with that last sentence there because if I didn't, you haven't been paying attention. I just told you that you *can't* control your feelings and that your meltdowns are automatic and reactive, and then I told you that you *can* control your behavior during an outburst. If it's all automatic, how the hell are you supposed to do that?

That's what the rest of this book is about. Don't worry, I'm not going to tell you that you should just choose to chill instead of losing your shit. If you coulda done that, you woulda done that, and I woulda done that, and we'd all be relaxing with Netflix and hot tea instead of looking for help in a book. Instead, I'm going to teach you how to reduce the likelihood that you will lose your shit by recognizing and responding effectively to your triggers, calming your buttons, and learning how to notice when you've been pushed too FAR so you don't let loose and go all toxic on your kiddo. Finally, I'm going to teach you exactly how to get your shit together after you've lost it so you don't lose it again.

Got it? Good. Now that we're clear on what it means to lose your shit, we need to talk about what it looks like when you don't.

What Does It Mean to Not Lose Your Shit?

· ·

Some folks think that the opposite of losing it is staying calm and collected all the time, and never getting into any sort of conflict with your child ever. They assume it means feeling happy, patient, and present at every moment, and responding to your children with a song in your heart and a smile on your face no matter what sort of crap (either metaphorical or literal) they dump at your exhausted feet. This sort of thinking just reeks of perfection and clearly won't work for me or you or any other parent on the planet.

Conflict and disconnection and unpleasant feelings and strong emotions are all completely normal and reasonable and acceptable, and *they don't mean you're doing anything wrong.* Living in close proximity with other people—who you may love dearly, even if you don't like everything they do—is not easy. It's especially challenging if one of you is chronically stressed and the other one is a small person with an immature brain. As a clinical social worker, I worry more about the folks who say they never fight than the ones who acknowledge and own the tension that exists in their families.

You can be overwhelmed by emotions and still not lose your shit. You can be deeply pissed off or scared or sad or confused, and still not reach a toxic level. You can let your kids know you're having Big Feelings without exploding all over them.

Not losing it is about having just enough self-awareness to notice what's going on in and around you so you can make a conscious

Finally, we're always modeling a way to behave, whether or not it's something we want our children to learn. Each time we lose it, we may be unintentionally wiring their brains and nervous systems to freak out in a similar way whenever they're triggered, perhaps by something that happens at school, at home, or inside their tiny little brains and bodies. We're demonstrating the very behaviors we're trying to decrease and we're modeling a relationship style we surely don't want them to repeat later in life. (Side note: This may be why you're struggling with this issue. If your parents lost it with you on a regular basis, they were inadvertently raising you to react similarly in stressful situations. Fortunately, you can break this intergenerational pattern.)

CALMER PARENTS MAKE FOR CALMER KIDS. Our temperament and energy levels help set the tone for the house. Every time we freak out, we raise the level of tension in our homes, which is exhausting and can create painful rifts in family connections. Alternately, the calmer we are, the calmer our kids might be. I'm not saying that you're 100 percent responsible for your children's behavior and energy level, and your Jedi mind tricks won't work all the time. However, to the extent that we can avoid adding fuel to their psychotic little fires, there will be a significant and noticeable difference for the entire family.

Having said all of that, I kind of get the appeal of losing your shit. It's quick, easy, and requires relatively little thought, and can we all 'fess up and admit that sometimes it feels good to stick it to the kid? What's more, it can be effective. Sort of. For a few minutes. It's certainly possible that if you scare the crap out of your children often enough, they'll do whatever you want just to keep you from losing it again. But walking on eggshells around someone is not the same as respecting them, and as soon as your kids are old enough to take some control over their time and space, they're going to react to you the same way you did the last time you worked for an explosive, unpredictable boss: AVOID. AVOID. AVOID. Once they disconnect from you in that way, parenting becomes a lot harder and less fun. While it's always possible to rebuild a relationship, that's a challenge you don't need.

Much of parenting is based on trust, which is an especially tricky issue for kids. They're wired to trust their parents and caregivers because we're the ones who are supposed to keep them safe. As a result, when we lose our shit with them, they tend to blame themselves because that's easier than questioning or doubting the person who keeps them alive and runs their lives. Over time, our kids may learn to not only tolerate and expect bad behavior in others but to also blame themselves for it.

Fortunately, it doesn't have to be that way. We respect the people we trust, the people who tend to treat us with kindness and honesty. When we respect people, we want to help them. We want to make them happy. We want to get home by curfew even though the party is really, really awesome. (OK, that's a total lie. Your kids won't want to leave that rockin' party, but they'll be much more likely to do it anyway *and* tell you about the guy who tried to get them to smoke a joint and what they did instead if they think they have a snowball's chance in hell at not getting reamed out the minute they walk in the door smelling like cheap beer.)

The reality is that our children learn more from what we do than from what we say, and their little kid brains don't necessarily make a distinction between our smart parenting moves and our terrible, impulsive ones. Every time we lose it we're not only demonstrating how to do the very thing we're trying to get them to stop doing, but we're actually wiring their brains to make it more likely that they do it again rather than wiring them for calm behavior and trust.

Why Is This So Hard?

I n order to change a behavior, it's helpful to get a handle on what's causing it in the first place. That's what our brains naturally want to do. The human mind loves a good story. Stories help us make sense of our experiences, understand the world around us, and feel connected and engaged with ourselves, our friends, and our community. But stories aren't just about understanding where we are and where we've been. Our stories are the maps of our lives, and the right story helps us figure out where we're going and how to get there.

Unfortunately, not every story is a good one. Our brains are so desperate to put the pieces together that they'll believe any tale, whether or not it's true or helpful. In the absence of accurate information, our minds will just make something up. Kids do this all the time; just the other day my daughter tried to tell me that she whacked her sister because she was remembering a joke about a monkey throwing a banana and her arm tried to throw a banana all on its own and it just happened to land right on her sister's nose. This, of course, was total BS. My kiddo had no idea why she hit her sister, but she's only eight, so instead of saying, "The thing is, Mommy, the part of my brain designed to help me control my

> We think our thoughts are The Truth, but the reality is that sometimes they are, and sometimes they're just mental monkeys throwing bananas.

impulses doesn't exist yet and that's why I hit my sister," she fed me a line. Our own brains feed us similar lines all the time.

Fortunately, most parents don't usually fall for their kids' insane stories, because they're, well, insane. Unfortunately, we generally believe most grown-ups' explanations, especially if those grown-ups (a) are wearing uniforms or have fancy letters after their names, (b) post them all over social media, or (c) happen to live inside our own minds. We fall for our own crap all the time. We think our thoughts are The Truth, but the reality is that sometimes they are, and sometimes they're just mental monkeys throwing bananas.

The stories we tell ourselves about why we keep losing it are a perfect example. The most common reasons I hear from my friends and clients are generally some variation of "I'm a bad parent" or "My kid is a jerk." It's easy to see why our brains come up with these explanations; they're logical enough. A good parent doesn't lose her shit, therefore the shit-losing parent is a bad one. Or perhaps it's that we don't lose it when the kids are being helpful and reasonable, so if we are losing our shit, it must be their fault. Makes sense, right?

Wrong. Because even if you think these stories are true (which, as I hope to convince you, they're not), the more important point is that they're not helpful.

Let's start with the bit about your kid being a jerk. There's no question that children's behavior can range from mildly annoying to mind-blowingly horrifying. They throw toys out the car window and refuse to nap and poop on the stairs and stomp on the baby's head and steal candy from the drugstore and draw penises on the classroom wall and don't even get me started on booze and drugs and sexting that punk with chin fuzz. Kids do idiotic, obnoxious stuff. That's unlikely to change any time soon, so if your plan for keeping your cool depends on your child's ability to do the same, that's going to end poorly for everyone. As you may have said to your kids a time or two, we can't control anyone else's behavior—we can only control our own.

So, let's talk about us.

Our behavior can be nearly as ridiculous as our kids' (although in my defense, I am an excellent napper and have never once pooped on the stairs). We make promises we can't keep and issue threats we have no intention of following through on; we hold our children to unreasonable expectations and then get supremely pissed off when they don't meet them; we set similarly unreasonable expectations for ourselves and then berate ourselves when we don't live up to them; and many of us rival our little ones in our tantrum-throwing abilities.

If your plan for keeping your cool depends on your child's ability to do the same, that's going to end poorly for everyone.

We all behave in ways that just don't make sense, especially when we're triggered and our buttons are pushed. But our brains start to get a little twitchy when things seem random or unpredictable; they prefer predictability, not chaos. This is why even

> Telling yourself that the reason you keep exploding is because you're a bad parent or you have a bad kid is an unhelpful story.

an inaccurate story can seem better than no story at all. When we don't have a clue about what just happened or what might happen next, we grasp (often without realizing it) at any available information to explain and understand the situation. Hence the "I'm a bad parent raising a bad kid" line.

Despite any and all evidence to the contrary, any explanation that starts or ends with you or your kid being a jerk ain't gonna cut it. I know what you're thinking here, and it's something like, "Oh, honey, if only you were a fly on the wall in my house, if you saw what goes down in my Casa de Crazy, you wouldn't be writing those words." The thing is, I have been a fly on the wall in many, many houses, as a child who grew up in a deeply dysfunctional family, as a parent who has lost her shit on her own kids on multiple occasions, and as a clinical social worker who has worked with, and been in the homes of, many families struggling with heartbreaking addiction, assault, abuse, and neglect. I know how bad it can get. And I still say that the bad parent / bad kid line doesn't work. Here's why.

Telling yourself that the reason you keep exploding is because you're a bad parent or you have a bad kid is an unhelpful story because it doesn't offer any options for change and growth. There's no movement, no fresh air, no possibility of a new perspective or different outcome. When you've already decided you're a bad parent, it can feel impossible to turn into a good one. You get stuck in the shame and have no idea where to start, and it all sucks and, oh well, maybe you can send the kid to boarding school or off to live with Aunt Louise in Sheboygan or divert some of their college money to a therapy/pharmaceutical/ashram fund.

Fortunately, there is another option. How about a new story, one that not only gives you a more accurate picture of what's actually happening but also offers a map for how to get to where you want to go? How about this one? *You're doing an incredibly hard job, and you're doing it without the right information, support, resources, and rest.* When we do something really hard every single day without those things, we lose it. It's the human way. We are literally wired to freak out when our buttons are repeatedly pushed. And I think we can all agree that parenting is nothing if not an exercise in repeated button pushing.

I talk about this with the parents I work with all the time. I remind them over and over again that raising children is insanely hard and that (a) it's not their fault that it's hard, and (b) they need to start doing what adults do in tough situations, like taking care of themselves and getting some help. They smile and nod and give me the old, "Yeah, yeah, I know. Can we please get back to my son's latest issue and what, exactly, I'm supposed to do about it?" And so I keep repeating myself, all the while imagining that I'm Robin Williams in that super-intense scene in *Good Will Hunting* where he keeps telling the traumatized Will, "It's not your fault. It's not your fault. It's not your fault." Eventually, Will breaks down in tears, presumably able to truly hear for the first time that his traumatic childhood is not his fault.

If for some unfathomable reason you haven't seen *Good Will Hunting*, go ahead and watch it now. Oh, wait. You can't because you're a parent and you don't have two free hours. So do the next best thing and google "good will hunting it's not your fault scene." Go ahead. I'll wait. Then imagine me with a beard, argyle cardigan, and Boston accent as you read this next paragraph.

You're *not* a bad parent, and while your shit losses are absolutely your responsibility, they're *not your fault*. This is a crucial distinction that bears repeating: There's no reason to blame yourself for your temper, but it's time to step up and make some changes. Remember, you're a mere human, trying to raise another mere human, which may be the hardest thing any of us ever do. It's hard at different times and in different ways for different parents, but it's hard for *everyone*. I promise. I double pinky swear.

WHY IS PARENTING SO DAMN HARD?

This is such an important question that we're going to take a moment to explore some of the reasons why parenting can be so challenging. Some of these reasons are universal and timeless, and some are specific to this generation of parenting and to you and your family. Understanding why parenting is so hard is a crucial first step toward dealing with it in a skillful way.

PARENTING IS HARD BECAUSE IT'S A PART OF LIFE, AND LIFE IS HARD. Our cultural obsession with happiness has created the false delusion that life should be easy and that we should be happy most, if not all, of the time. The carefully curated and filtered world of social media further perpetuates this BS idea that there are folks out there who effortlessly have their lives together in a consistent, ongoing way. The end result is that those of us (which is actually all of us) who have to deal with flat tires and debilitating anxiety and dwindling bank accounts and difficult family members and ingrown toenails are left thinking that everyone else has figured it out and we're the ones doing something wrong.

Every time I come across the Life Is Happy lie, I imagine my great-grandmother, a tough old bullfrog of a woman who lived through the Oklahoma Land Rush. I have a picture of her sitting on a dusty stoop in front of a log cabin, and you can just see the challenges of her life etched into the deep wrinkles on her face. If she could hear the advice of today's positive-thinking gurus, she'd probably think back on everything she'd been through (most of which I can't even imagine), laugh her ass off, and then tell them to take their happiness crap and get the hell off her land.

> Remember, you're a mere human, trying to raise another mere human, which may be the hardest thing any of us ever do.

Life is hard. Sure, there are things we can do to make it a bit easier, and if we're lucky, we string together a few good days and a few good years and that's not nothing. Parenting is no different. If parenting and life are feeling particularly challenging for any reason, it's not always because you're doing something wrong. It's because hard is part of the deal for everyone, no matter how good they make it look on Instagram.

YOUR LIFE CIRCUMSTANCES CAN MAKE PARENTING HARDER.

Raising children can be brutal, even for folks who are physically and emotionally healthy, have supportive partners and family, and don't have to worry about how they're going to cover their bills next month.

But it's especially challenging if you're unemployed, underemployed, financially stressed, homeless, parenting without a partner, living with addiction or violence, mourning a loss, caring for aging loved ones, managing physical or mental illness, raising a child with special needs, or dealing with conflict or drama with your friends or family members. Some of these problems will pass, and some of them will continue to add stress to your life for the foreseeable future. But they all trigger us, and when we're triggered, we're more likely to lose our shit.

YOUR CHILDHOOD CAN MAKE PARENTING HARDER. If you grew up in a home with addiction, violence, loss, abuse, or neglect of any sort, it's going to impact your parenting, and probably not in a good way. This can happen for a lot of reasons, including:

★ You may be more likely to struggle with post-traumatic stress disorder, anxiety, depression, addiction, or chronic illnesses, any of which will interfere with your ability to parent your kids the way you want to.

★ If you haven't yet made sense of your childhood and how it impacts your adult life, the early lessons you learned about how families work and parents behave may rear their ugly heads in ways that you don't even realize. Seemingly small moments that barely register on other folks' radar can trigger you, and all of a sudden you're screaming even though you don't know why.

★ Your family of origin may be an ongoing source of stress in your life, which is a double whammy because it also means they aren't available to offer you the support and assistance that can be so useful from grandparents and other family members.

★ You don't have a model for how you want to parent, which is kind of like building a house without a blueprint. Chances are you're going to end up with a fairly confusing and uncomfortable house, one that you never feel quite comfortable navigating.

> Seemingly small moments that barely register on other folks' radar can trigger you, and all of a sudden you're screaming even though you don't know why.

Even if your early years weren't traumatic, the experience of being underparented or parented in ways that you don't want to replicate will make it harder for you to figure out how you do want to raise your kids. Not knowing what to do can increase your stress, which makes parenting harder.

SOME KIDS ARE HARDER TO PARENT. Some babies sleep through the night. Some kids figure out how to walk and talk and solve geometry proofs at the same pace as all the other kids on the block. Some kids are chill and flexible, some kids actually enjoy following rules, some kids just freak out less often than others. Other children struggle with insomnia, chronic illnesses, or learning disabilities. And other children are constantly distracted, or they have Big Feelings that they express in loud and unpleasant ways in very public spaces, or they require years of therapy and tutoring, or they were highstrung from the moment they emerged from the womb.

And some children, regardless of their temperament or temper are, quite simply, a better fit for their parents. Their style, whether they're early birds or night owls, loud or quiet, adventure seekers or homebodies, matches well with the rest of the family. And some kids just don't. The painful truth that no one wants to talk about is that some kids are just harder to parent.

MOST PARENTS SUCK AT TAKING CARE OF THEMSELVES. I'm sure you've read more than a few listicles explaining all the reasons you should be taking better care of yourself and all of the ways to do it: Pedicures and Pinot with the ladies! Trivia night! Train for a marathon! (Ugh. Ugh. Double ugh.) As long as we're on the topic of marathons, though, they do make a great metaphor for parenting. Those of you who have actually run a marathon know that you're unlikely to perform at your best if (a) your training runs keep getting interrupted by calls from the school nurse, (b) your carbo-loading consists of inhaling the remnants of your kids' mac 'n' cheese, and (c) you haven't slept through the night for nearly a decade. Runners who know they haven't been able to properly prepare their bodies lower their expectations and cut themselves some slack when the race doesn't go as well as they had hoped.

Yet most parents do nothing of the sort. Whether you're home full-time, working outside the house, or doing some hybrid of the two, you're absolutely running a marathon every day, and you need as many hours of rest and recuperation as you spend parenting. (HAHAHAHA *SOB*) But are you even coming close? How often do you get eight hours of sleep? Are you moving your body regularly? When was the last time you had a day or a morning

> The painful truth that no one wants to talk about is that some kids are just harder to parent.

or even an hour free to read a book or go for a walk or do something just for fun? (For the record, zoning out on the couch in exhausted-zombie mode with your tablet in your lap and Netflix on the TV at the end of the day doesn't count.) And even if you can point to a fortunate afternoon last weekend when the stars aligned and all of your children were out to playdates at the same time, I'm betting it doesn't happen on a regular basis. Too many parents move through their days running on fumes, exhausted, stressed-out, overcaffeinated, and poorly fed, and yet still hold themselves to the same high standards and berate themselves for their "bad parenting" when they don't measure up.

CHRONIC EXHAUSTION MAKES PARENTING HARDER. Sleep is so crucial that it gets an extra special nod here. The majority of parents I work with are exhausted. Fatigue makes it harder to think clearly, solve even the most basic problems, focus our attention, manage our emotions, make good choices, and stay healthy. Basically, when we go too long without enough sleep, we become the worst version of ourselves. We get cranky and bitchy and reactive and we are far more likely to lose it. And no, you can't think or work or willpower your way out of exhaustion because the very part of your brain that's responsible for that kind of adulting is the first part of your brain to shut down when you've been up all night with a sick kid. So that stinks.

MOST OF US ARE RAISING OUR CHILDREN WITHOUT ENOUGH SUPPORT, OR WITH THE WRONG KIND OF SUPPORT. I recently had dinner with some folks from Canada and my jaw hit the floor as my pregnant friend described the year—YEAR!—of paid maternity leave she would enjoy before going back to the job that her employer was required to hold for her. Then she started throwing around phrases like "government-supported childcare" and "guaranteed health care" and I nearly choked. The current American system has very real implications for our lives; the daily grind of rushing from childcare drop-off to work and back again, perpetually on the verge of running out of time and money, is stressful and exhausting.

The lack of support is not just a problem on the systemic level; it's a problem on a local level as well. As folks move away from home for schools or jobs, they're also moving away from their families. Sometimes that's a good thing, but it also means we're losing the communities that once guided us in how to raise children. Yes, those villages may have been the source of some epically crappy advice (Put orange juice in the baby's bottle! Spank them! Ditch the seat belts—kids need their physical freedom!), but at least that advice came wrapped in a package of "Well, that's how everyone did it." There is great comfort in the knowledge that if we're making poor parenting choices, at least we're doing it together.

The lack of support is not just a problem on the systemic level; it's a problem on a local level as well.

The customs of our local villages have been replaced by an endless stream of advice from the global village, thanks to the power of the Internet. Instead of taking comfort in the fact that we're not the only ones stumbling through parenting, we're constantly reminded that we're the only ones who *aren't* getting it right. The attachment parents are attaching better, the French moms are feeding their kids better, the Scandinavian kids are happier, the Asian kids are smarter and harder working, and meanwhile I'm just trying to figure out how to get my kid to stop picking her nose and wiping it on the wall.

SOCIAL MEDIA AND SMARTPHONES MAKE PARENTING HARDER.

I enjoy social media as much as the next smartphone-addicted, update-obsessed, overly-prone-to-comparisons parent. But the constant updates make life harder in significant ways. Images of perfectly frosted birthday cupcakes and videos of six-year-olds playing their first piano recitals make us doubt ourselves and our parenting choices and abilities, which, you guessed it, is a major trigger for most folks.

But it's not just the constant comparisons. Every time we open up Facebook or Twitter, we risk coming across distressing news, whether political or local or a tragic update from a high school friend. Those of us who grew up in the age of CNN and the twenty-four-hour news cycle fail to realize how truly insane this is. We are often unaware that this level of exposure to all of the terrible things that are happening in every corner of the planet is incredibly anxiety-provoking.

Example: I had to reset my smartphone the other day, and I forgot to turn off notifications when I restarted it. Generally, the only time my phone lights up or dings is for calls or text messages. I was making dinner when the screen flashed and the phone vibrated on the counter. The headline said something about the president declaring a state of emergency, at which point the text was cut off. I freaked out. Something terrible was happening. An earthquake? An invasion? An invasion of what? The body snatchers? What are body snatchers anyway?

It took me several deeply agitated minutes—during which time I totally snapped at my daughters—to calm down and figure out what was actually going on. I breathed deeply and checked the phone again. The president was declaring a state of emergency about the opioid crisis. Oh. Huh. Yes, addiction is a big deal, but it wasn't going to send me and the girls scurrying to the basement any time soon. I took several more deep breaths, apologized to my kids, and immediately turned off all the notifications.

TOO MUCH INFORMATION FROM TOO MANY EXPERTS MAKES PARENTING HARDER. This may sound a bit rich coming from a parent coach who has written three parenting books, but hear me out. There is a ton of excellent advice out there that makes parenting easier. But there is also a tipping point at which the information becomes overwhelming and unhelpful, and not just because it can be inconsistent and constantly changing. No peanut butter before age one! All the peanut butter before age one! No screen time! Some screen time! No, not *that* much screen time!

In addition, all that advice creates the illusion that we can fix any parenting problem that comes our way, even though some of the most common problems just aren't fixable, not even with the prettiest star charts or the smartest words said in the perfect tone of voice at just the right time or the advice of the most accomplished child psychologist your side of the Mississippi. Some problems are just part of the imperfect life we imperfect humans are living, and the best we can do is muddle through, ideally with a hefty dose of compassion and the help of a good friend who will make you a snack and keep you laughing even when it feels like it's all falling apart. But that's hard to hear and even harder to accept because we parents have been led to believe that it's our job to ensure our children's happiness. So we keep reading and researching and consulting and working our asses off, and we take whatever advice we can. But when it doesn't work, we end up thinking we've failed at parenting rather than realizing that the advice has failed us.

OK. Whew. Now that I've dropped you into the depths of despair about how rough parenting can be, it's time to pick you up, dust you off, and get you back in the game. Remember, you're not a bad parent raising a bad kid. Life is hard and parenting is hard. It's not your fault you're losing your shit, but it's absolutely your responsibility to do what you can to reduce the likelihood that you will lose it and to stay cool as often as possible. On the off chance you're having a little pity party right now, well, go ahead (we all do it sometimes) and then keep reading because taking responsibility for shit that's not your fault is what parenting is all about. Let's get to it.

Why We Lose It When Shit Gets Hard

t first glance, it may seem as though the whole "parenting is hard" shtick is just another unhelpful story; after all, if it's so challenging, then what's the point of even talking about it? The point is that understanding the nature of the challenges we face is the first step toward change. The next step is understanding why we lose our shit when shit gets hard, and it's all about your brain and nervous system.

There is no question that the human brain is awesome; it gave us *Grey's Anatomy* and Velcro sneakers and broccoli you can steam right in the bag. Unfortunately, it can also lead us astray in some pretty major ways. I'm guessing that no one ever gave you the instruction manual on how your brain develops and works, how to take care of it, and what exactly happens when you don't. Now, in their defense (I'm not entirely sure who "they" are, but roll with me on this one), they hadn't yet figured it out themselves. But now we're starting to get a decent handle on brain science and what might be going on when we lose it.

Right off the bat, there are a few things you need to know about your nervous system, which includes your brain, spinal cord, and the nerves that run throughout your body. One of these is that your brain is made up of many different parts. Those parts are responsible for various aspects of your functioning, and they all have ridiculous names that you don't need to remember. There are a few parts of your brain that are relevant to your shit loss, though; we'll focus on two of them.

> The calmer we can get (and stay), the calmer our kids will be as well.

First, your prefrontal cortex (PFC). This lives right behind your forehead, and it's the part of your brain that comes online when you're adulting. Your PFC helps you plan ahead, make decisions, think logically and creatively, manage your feelings, and calm down when you're freaking out. Two things you need to know about it: First, it gets tired when it has to work too hard for too long, which is why it can feel impossible to figure out what to make for dinner at the end of a long day. Second, certain practices (which generally fall under the umbrella of self-care) will make your PFC more effective and efficient so it can get you through the day without falling apart.

One more fun little factoid about the PFC: Your kids don't really have one yet. The latest thinking is that the PFC isn't fully developed until the early twenties, which is why even college students are still lighting stuff on fire for no good reason. Having said that, all is not lost. The calmer we can get (and stay), the calmer our kids will be as well. Basically, our PFCs are functioning for theirs.

What, you say? My child doesn't have a prefrontal cortex? If that's true, then what part of their brain is running that crazy little show? Great question! For the purposes of oversimplification, it's their limbic system. You also have a limbic system. It's tucked away inside the middle of your brain, and it includes the amygdala, hippocampus, and hypothalamus, and all of the neuronal highways their information travels on. (I told you they have ridiculous names.) Your limbic system has a few different functions, but for now, just think of it as your inner toddler. It's responsible for your Big Feelings, and it triggers your Fight, Flight, Freeze, or Freak Out reaction. (In the event that you've forgotten how good toddlers are at freaking out, just go tear a cheese stick the wrong way.) The limbic system takes over when your PFC goes off-line for any reason, including exhaustion, Big Feelings, real or perceived threats, being overwhelmed, or having your buttons pushed. Needless to say, your limbic system plays a major role in shit-loss–related situations.

Although we all have PFCs and limbic systems, they're wired a little differently depending on the person. They can be bigger or smaller, and more or less active, for a variety of reasons. Brain development (which includes both structure and function) is influenced by a ton of different factors, including genetics, gender, illness, life experience, education, traumatic incidences, and random shit that scientists have yet to figure out.

Fortunately, you're not stuck with what you've got now. The human brain changes and grows throughout your life. Many new parents get super hung up about the first three years being the height of brain development—if you don't expose Little Susie to enough Baby Mozart and kale before she heads off to preschool, you've screwed her for life! This is an unhelpful story for every single person on the planet who is older than three, and it's not true, so let's ditch it. The truth is that there is a lot of activity in those early years, and another truth is that our brains continue to learn and develop, in both helpful and unhelpful ways, as long as we're alive.

> Your thoughts and feelings impact and change how your body feels and functions.

In addition, the human brain wasn't designed to be maximally effective at all times. It was designed (a) to keep us alive, and (b) to plan and remember and worry and anticipate and imagine and fantasize and think and react, mostly in the service of (a) keeping us alive. Those little neurons fire like it's their job, because, well, it's their job. Sometimes all of this brain activity is helpful, but sometimes it's not. Sometimes our thoughts, ideas, and reactions are accurate and useful, and sometimes they steer us in the wrong direction. We can't depend on our brains to guide us like a thoughtful parent or therapist; evolution just didn't design them that way.

Although evolution might not have wired our brains to be super wise all the time, it did wire them to keep us breathing and moving, thanks to our nervous system. There are nerves all over your body, and each time they sense something, they send messages back to your brain. In the same way, your thoughts and feelings send messages throughout your nervous system and into your body. They don't exist in a vacuum; your thoughts and feelings impact and change how your body feels and functions. This happens constantly and even more quickly than you can imagine, often without you having a clue.

Your brain (and thus, your nervous system) is not self-sustaining. It requires sleep, nutrition, exercise, stimulation, fun, and downtime to function well. It's like one of those little digital pets that used to be so popular; as long as you tend to it, it will beep and smile when it should and generally behave well most of the time. And when you don't tend to your brain, things like parenting become harder and you become much more likely to lose your shit.

One last point: While your brain is not a muscle, it's useful to think about it as if it is. The more you use certain parts, the stronger they get, and the more likely they will be to come online the next time you need them. Have you ever watched a kid the first time they get on the soccer field? They can barely get their foot to connect with the ball. With enough practice, though, they can dribble the ball down the field without a second thought.

The opposite is also true. The less frequently you activate certain parts of your brain, the weaker and more rigid they become. This is why it's harder to learn an instrument or language later in life; the neuronal pathways we need are just too rusty to make those new connections quickly and easily. (This doesn't mean they can't; it's just harder.)

Furthermore, our brains don't make a distinction between the skillful "muscles" that you might actually want to make stronger and the shittier "muscles" that you probably wish didn't exist at all.

Basically, you'll get better at whatever you're practicing, whether it's meditating or melting down. I practiced yelling for years, and man, I got really good at it. Fortunately, once I started noticing when I was about to lose it and chose to shut my mouth and breathe deeply instead, I got a lot better at that. Over time, it became easier and easier to do.

WHAT YOUR NERVOUS SYSTEM HAS TO DO WITH YOUR SHIT LOSS

By now you're probably wondering what this all has to do with you and your temper. It's all about your Fight or Flight response, which I prefer to think of as Fight, Flight, Freeze, or Freak Out.

When some part of your nervous system senses—either consciously or unconsciously, accurately or not—that Something Big and Possibly Bad is happening or might happen, it immediately sends a warning to your limbic system, which then activates your sympathetic nervous system. Your body is flooded with stress hormones, which trigger a series of reactions. Your heart starts pounding, your blood pressure shoots up, you start breathing harder and faster, your muscles tighten, you may start shaking or trembling, and your pupils dilate. This can happen so quickly and subtly at times that you might not even notice.

These aren't random reactions; they're specifically designed to keep you safe by preparing you to kick ass, freeze up, or sprint away. If you can't do any of these things, perhaps because you're stuck at home with a toddler and a newborn, all of that tension and energy may get diverted into a parental explosion instead.

At the same time, your sympathetic nervous system also shuts down the "unnecessary" systems in your body so it can divert the energy to where it's most needed. Unfortunately, those allegedly unnecessary systems include your prefrontal cortex, the adulting part of your brain. This totally made sense when our brains were still developing; if a woolly mammoth was coming at you, you didn't need to stop and invent the wheel. You needed to run, and you didn't need your PFC to help you do that.

Many folks assume we only go all 4F (Fight, Flight, Freeze, or Freak Out) when there's a bear chasing us or a car driving straight at us, but the truth is that our nervous system can react quickly to almost anything—from the sight of our kid climbing too high at the playground to a jump rope on the sidewalk that looks like a snake but is really just a rope. As any parent who has grabbed a tiny hand away from a hot stove can tell you, it can all happen in a matter of seconds.

There's just one problem with all of this evolutionary awesomeness. Our survival system evolved in response to physical threats such as the aforementioned woolly mammoth, which is why our reaction is almost entirely physical. But times have changed and most of the threats we now face are psychological, such as rude colleagues, intrusive in-laws, and late-night panic attacks about the concerning email from our child's teacher. Sadly, our nerves and brains and everything in between haven't quite figured that out, which is why we still have physical reactions to situations that pose no physical threat at all. This automatic reaction can literally save our lives, but it can also cause us to lose our shit unnecessarily.

The brains of parents may be even more finely tuned to potential dangers than those of folks who don't have kids. Evolutionarily speaking, it makes sense. The cave moms and dads who tended toward the paranoid and vigilant may have been more likely to detect and respond to threats to their offspring, making them more likely to survive and procreate, thus passing along the nervous wiring that kept them alive in the first place. The super-chill cave parents may have been so busy carving happy faces into the wall that they didn't notice their cave child wander away right into the waiting jaws of a saber-toothed tiger, thus killing off the chill gene along with any hope we may have once had at not losing it with our kids.

As I've mentioned before, I want you to think of your nervous system as a bunch of buttons all over your body. I'm not talking about the buttons that keep popping off your kid's sweater; I'm talking about your big red ones, just aching to be pushed. (This, of course, is in no way physiologically accurate, but for the purposes of this book, it works.) When we're calm, fed, well rested, appropriately caffeinated, etc., our buttons are small, dim, less sensitive, and generally less vulnerable to being pushed. That's not to say they are totally pushproof; anyone who has been in a car accident or been awakened in the middle of the night by the screeching of a smoke alarm or a small child knows that our nervous system can go from zero to sixty in the course of a few seconds. But for most of us, that's not how it happens most of the time.

Think of your nervous system as a bunch of buttons all over your body.

More commonly, we're exposed to smaller triggers over time, and our buttons slowly get bigger, brighter, more sensitive, and easier for our kids to push. Our baseline functioning gets elevated, bringing us closer in general to losing it. The more triggered we are, the more our limbic system amps up, ready to send us into reactive mode, until we get to the point where it just takes one thrown toy or smart-ass comment to send us over the edge. The limbic system takes control, the prefrontal cortex goes off-line, and shit is lost.

> When we're calm, fed, well rested, appropriately caffeinated, etc., our buttons are small, dim, less sensitive, and generally less vulnerable to being pushed.

Fortunately for the sanity of everyone involved, the opposite is also true. Each time we get enough sleep, move our bodies, stretch, breathe, spend time with friends, do a crossword puzzle, read a book, and take care of ourselves in basic ways, we're calming those buttons down. We're activating our parasympathetic nervous system (the relaxation and connection part of our nervous system), strengthening our prefrontal cortexes, and lowering our overall baseline, bringing us closer to a place of chill. Basically, we're creating more space between our current state and freaking out. But if we don't take care of ourselves properly, our buttons never really power down. And for those of us dealing with constant chaos or chronic stressors, it can be harder (but not impossible) to get our system to cool off in a consistent way.

Wrapping It Up

We've talked about a lot in this chapter, so here's a quick recap. We all lose it with our kids, and most of our parenting meltdowns share a few common features. There are lots of Big **F**eelings involved, and our behavior is **A**utomatic, **R**eactive, and **T**oxic. Not losing our shit doesn't mean our hearts and homes are filled with rainbows and baby unicorns, it just means we find skillful ways to manage the conflicts and express the unpleasant emotions that arise. And arise they will, because parenting is hard, and it's even harder when you're doing it without the right information, resources, rest, and support. The challenges of parenting and life can be incredibly triggering, making our buttons (aka our nervous system) bigger, brighter, and way easier for our kids to push. We all get triggered; it's not a personal weakness or moral failing. It's just part of what it means to be human. I've been so triggered at times that my sweet girls needed only to glance in my general direction in order to push my buttons, and next thing I knew, I was snapping at them to stop looking at me. In case it's not clear to you, dear reader, this was not a pro parenting move.

Fortunately, the rest of this book is all about pro parenting moves. It will help you get a handle on what triggers you, how to manage those triggers whenever possible, and how to take care of yourself when you can't. We're also going to explore what to do when you've done everything you can and you're still on the edge, or you've already fallen off that cliff and you have no idea how to peel yourself off the ground and get it together.

But first, we're going to talk about me.

CHAPTER 2

How I Stopped Losing My Shit (Quite So Often)

MY SHIT-LOSING DAYS IN ALL THEIR GLORY

★

HOW I GOT IT TOGETHER AGAIN

Hopefully, by now you're in a good mind-set to successfully tackle the practices in the rest of this book. If you're still blaming or shaming yourself or struggling with Bad Parent BS, reread Chapter 1 and go spend some time with people who love you and can remind you that (1) you're awesome, (2) parenting is hard for everyone, (3) you're gonna screw it up (it's inevitable), and (4) you're still awesome.

Let me repeat that: Screwing up and being awesome are *not* mutually exclusive.

I also hope that you're eager for some more information about how to not lose it with your kids, and we'll get to that soon, I promise. But if information were all we needed to make hard changes, the tobacco industry would be bankrupt and we'd all be hitting the gym at sunrise and drinking kale smoothies for breakfast. Advice is just one piece of the change puzzle. When you can let go of embarrassment, shame, and guilt, you'll feel freer and

> Screwing up and being awesome are not mutually exclusive.

more empowered to do things differently. It all starts with the sense of empathy, understanding, and acceptance that can only come from connecting with parents who have been there and really get how rough it can be. Knowing that you're not alone—that you're not the only one who has felt intense rage or frustration or disappointment at your kids, who has lost control or exploded at them in ways that surprised even you—is crucial to changing old habits and creating new ones. That's what I'm here for. Whenever you feel overwhelmed or stressed out, read this chapter and remember that I'm also a perfectly imperfect parent, and we're all in this together.

Right off the bat, you need to know that I didn't do any of this alone. I would not have gotten my shit together without support from my husband, friends, family, therapist, and doctors. It was hard to admit how much I was struggling, but the more I talked with folks I trusted, the easier it got. Don't think you're going to get everything you need by reading this book. Find your peeps and let them help you.

Getting my shit together wasn't pretty. There were no magic pills, no spa retreats, no overnight transformation.

Getting my shit together wasn't pretty. There were no magic pills, no spa retreats, no overnight transformation. I gained weight. I ended up on medication and in therapy. The process took time. It wasn't always easy, but I came out on the other side, and so can you.

Even now, it's an ongoing process. I still get anxious and stressed, and I still lose it sometimes, which means I need to stay on top of all the shit I need to do so I don't lose my shit. For me, this means caffeinating and meditating, getting in bed by 10 p.m. each night, and exercising daily, generally by going for walks in my neighborhood or doing a yoga video in my bedroom with a needy-ass cat messing with my downward dog. The instruction manual for the Care and Keeping of Carla has gotten thicker and more detailed since I became a parent, but the more I stick to it, the easier and more fun parenting and life are.

Why I Was Losing My Shit
THE TRIGGERS OF PARENTHOOD

first attempted to get my shit together on that night I mentioned back in the Introduction. My daughters were little, maybe two and three years old, and we were having a rough evening. They didn't listen, I got frustrated and snapped at them, they started crying, I felt awful, they didn't listen again, I yelled again, they cried more, and well, you know where this is going. Eventually, I gave up and put them in front of a cartoon. Turning on the TV only compounded my shame because I worried that (a) I was rewarding them for their crappy behavior (although in retrospect, their crappy behavior was as much a response to my crappy behavior as anything else) and (b) the screen time was probably frying their little brain cells when they should have been building towers with handcrafted wooden blocks. It was better than the stress of my relentless yelling, I reasoned, and even if it wasn't, I didn't know what else to do. I put them on the couch with a soft blanket and their loveys while I sat down at the computer and googled "how to stop yelling at my kids." I then made a list of Everything I Was Going to Do Instead of Yelling. I was ready to change.

Within a day or two I had lost it again, but this time I carried the bonus burden of feeling guilty about my temper *and* my failure to stick to my plan. How had all of these other parents figured out the secret to staying calm and happy while I could barely make it a day without screaming? (News flash: They hadn't.) What was wrong with me? (Update: Nothing. This isn't a moral failing.) Why couldn't I stay calm, patient, and connected to my kids in difficult moments? (Hint: Because I didn't yet have the right information and support.) And even if I couldn't do that, why couldn't I just shut my damn mouth and not yell? (Answer: Because even that small feat can be much harder than it sounds.)

I couldn't see it then, but I know now that my short temper, impatience, frustration, and yelling weren't the problems. Yes, of course, they were problems, but more importantly, they were symptoms. They were my brain and body's response to being constantly triggered. Looking back, I can identify four primary triggers.

BECOMING A PARENT. A few hours after my daughter was born, I called my grandfather with the good news. "Well," he said in a gravelly voice, "it's a crisis, but you'll get through it." I wasn't sure what to make of his response, so I wrote it off as the rambling of a cranky old man. Now I realize he was the only one speaking the truth. The daily grind of caring for infants and toddlers is absolutely a crisis, and a brutal adjustment for most folks, including yours truly. Children are needy and unpredictable and inconvenient, and I wasn't prepared for any of it.

Becoming a parent rattled my entire life, including my academic studies, my career plans, and my relationships. I expected motherhood to be challenging; I didn't expect it to turn everything upside down. It was as though I was back in my freshman year of college, trying to make new friends and figure out what I wanted to do with my life and every time I turned around someone was vomiting. Except now *I* was supposed to be the adult.

To complicate things even more, my own childhood had been chaotic, characterized by multiple divorces, substance abuse, mental illness, lots of screaming, and extended periods of separation from both my mother and father. Despite the fact that I was now the parent, being back in the parent-child relationship triggered me in a variety of ways, most of which I was completely unaware of. I knew I was freaking out, but I didn't know why.

ANXIETY. In late October of 2008, I came home with a healthy baby and a hefty case of postpartum anxiety, of which I was completely unaware (the anxiety, that is, not the baby). I was perpetually freaked out, to the point that I started bumping down our hardwood stairs on my butt because I was worried about slipping and falling with my daughter in my arms.

I remember one night in particular when she was about six months old. Like every other night since she was born, I snuck into her room before I went to sleep to make sure she was still breathing. And, like every other night, her little chest was rising and falling in a slow, steady rhythm. I tiptoed out, closed the door, and got into bed. Almost immediately, I imagined a scenario in which my daughter had stopped breathing and I had to call 911. The paramedics would come racing in through the front door, but they would trip over all the shoes and winter clothes piled up on the stairs in our tiny entranceway. They wouldn't be able to get to the baby in time—all because I didn't clean up.

I must have lain there for hours, convinced that I should go tidy up, while also worrying that doing so would awaken my husband, who was as worn out I was. Besides, I knew my daughter was fine and there wouldn't be an ambulance screeching into our driveway any time soon. Even so, the thought kept returning—the terrible, horrifying possibility that perhaps my daughter had in fact stopped breathing at some point during my late-night freak-out and I should probably check on her because how ironic would that be, in the worst possible way, of course? But getting out of bed would be tantamount to admitting how out of control my own thoughts and feelings had become. I tried to convince myself that everything was OK, but instead I just lay there, imagining several burly EMTs in their blue uniforms, tripping over snow boots and sneakers and tiny pink moccasins as they raced up our stairs to get to my motionless baby. That went about as well as you'd think. I didn't sleep that night and on many other nights. My mind was constantly filled with images and worries about everything awful that could possibly happen to my baby.

MEDICAL CRISES. In my first few years of motherhood, members of my family dealt with a variety of medical issues, including fractures, burns, chronic ear infections requiring ear tubes, and seemingly endless cases of the croup (a viral infection that leads to throat swelling, a barky cough, and, in the worst cases, difficulty breathing). A close family member ended up in the ICU due to a bad medication reaction (thankfully, she's fine now).

Oh, and remember how I butt-slid down the stairs because I was scared of falling? Yeah. That. When my daughter was six, she fell down the stairs, and by the time she hit the bottom, her arm was fractured. I'm not sure if that was before or after the time her school had to call 911 because of an asthma attack.

You have to be freaking kidding me.

Through it all, I tried to remember how lucky we were, lucky that most of the injuries and illnesses were relatively minor and that we had health insurance and access to high-quality medical care. What I didn't stop to consider was how triggered I was by all of it. My anxiety continued to explode, and I was increasingly worried about my daughters' health and safety. Over time the constant hypervigilance wore me down, stressed me out, and put me at high risk of losing my shit.

EXHAUSTION. Intellectually, I knew how bad sleep deprivation is for every aspect of functioning. I spent the early years of my social work career working on an inpatient psychiatric unit, and I

> Rather than honestly acknowledging how tired I was and how my fatigue was impacting my daily functioning, I wore it like a badge of pride.

had witnessed the crucial role sleep plays in calming chaotic thoughts and explosive emotions. I just didn't make the connection to my own situation. Rather than honestly acknowledging how tired I was and how my fatigue was impacting my daily functioning, I wore it like a badge of pride. I was doing it all, and I had my trusty coffee and dark circles under my eyes to prove it.

Except I wasn't doing it all. I struggled through each day with the help of caffeine and sugar, and eventually fell into a cycle of eating my way through the day and worrying my way through the night. Over the course of five years, I gained a significant amount of weight. I was diagnosed with sleep apnea, an increasingly common disorder in which people stop breathing for brief periods of time during the night. The sleep disruptions happened so quickly and subtly that I wasn't even aware of them, but they interrupted my sleep enough that I often woke up exhausted after what I thought was a decent night of rest.

I can see now how my triggers—becoming a parent, anxiety, medical crises, and exhaustion—colluded to totally overwhelm me. But I was too tired and too overwhelmed to get any perspective on my situation. Instead, I decided it was a matter of willpower and determination. I became obsessed with self-help books and parenting advice in hopes of preventing or fixing anything that might go wrong. I didn't let my guard down, which is a slightly less crazy way of saying I became a walking, talking bright red button, just waiting to be pushed. Unfortunately for my sanity, I was spending the majority of my waking hours with two little button pushers.

I was always thinking and planning and anticipating. How many nights in a row of boxed mac 'n' cheese are too many? When should I start worrying about the thumb sucking? Is the baby colorblind? Should I be playing more classical music for them? What brand of probiotics should I be giving them? Should I worry about the fact that they both write backward? (Yes, I even worried about what to worry about. That's some highly advanced anxiety right there, folks.)

Our babysitter once responded to my litany of instructions and updates by smiling and saying, "Wow. It must be exhausting to live in your brain." Oh honey, I remember thinking, you have no idea. And then I proceeded to worry about whether I had become one of those naggy, hypervigilant helicopter parents I so desperately didn't want to be.

I realize now that I focused on the smaller stuff because the big stuff—primarily around the health and safety of my children and other family members—was just too overwhelming. I couldn't focus or concentrate, and I was forgetting, breaking, dropping, and losing things regularly. I was falling behind in my dissertation and, later, my book deadlines. I was getting less and less sleep, gaining more and more weight, and taking it all out on my kids. No matter how often I swore to myself that I wasn't going to yell at them at again, nothing was changing.

I was losing my shit. A lot.

How I Actually Got My Shit Together

U ltimately, it wasn't willpower or the advice of gurus that helped me get my shit together. Nothing changed until I finally listened to the one person who knows me best: my husband. He had been saying for months that he thought I had a sleep disorder, and I refused to listen because honestly, who actually listens to their spouse? But he was persistent, so I scheduled an appointment with a sleep doctor, which ultimately led to a diagnosis and treatment that helped me sleep soundly more often than not.

Sleeping again was the first crucial step toward getting my shit together, because it gave me the energy to take the next steps. The more I slept, the less irritable and reactive I was with my kids. I was also less likely to drive off with my favorite travel mug full of coffee balanced precariously on the roof of my car. (And yes, I was still drinking coffee. Let's not get carried away here, people.) I was more productive at work and thus felt like less of a professional failure. I had the

> Sleeping again was the first crucial step toward getting my shit together.

energy to start exercising. Although I didn't realize it at the time, sleeping, exercising, and sorting out my work life all helped me calm my nervous system, cool my buttons, and make me less likely to freak out at my kids.

It also gave me the energy and motivation to get back into therapy.

Oh, therapy. Therapy is one of those words that experts toss around like glitter, which looks shiny from a distance but becomes super overwhelming the closer you get to it. As much as I love glitter (which is actually not at all; have you ever tried to clean that shit up?), I'd like to offer something a little more substantial. So, here, in no particular order, is a list of all the ways in which therapy helped me. (For the record, you can also get many of these benefits from conversations with trusted clergy members, counselors, coaches, and doctors, and at parenting support groups, among other places.)

★ **It gave me a place to lose my shit without feeling like I was losing my shit all over the place.** I have found few experiences to be more liberating than going into a room with a person you trust and laying bare the worst sides of yourself and ugly-crying, and knowing the other person is really listening and isn't judging you even one bit and then—wait for it, here comes the best part—walking out of the room and hearing the door close behind you, knowing that you left your shit back there and you don't have to visit it again until next Wednesday at 2 p.m.

★ **I got clarity and insight into my parenting challenges.** You'd think that as a mental-health professional I'd be able to figure this stuff out on my own. Wrong. I was the lazy gym teacher of parenting, great at giving advice but not so good at heeding it myself. My therapist and I talked about my childhood, which helped me understand how my buttons developed the way they did, and which dynamics and behaviors are most likely to light them up and push them now. This helped me understand situations that had previously felt out of control and unpredictable, including losing my shit with my kids.

★ **My therapist gave me perspective.** One of the major challenges of being an anxious self-help junkie in the age of twenty-four-hour news, parenting experts, and social media is that I was constantly exposed to everyone's (often contradictory and/or unfounded) opinions about what I should and shouldn't be doing and all of the ways in which I will deeply screw up my kids if I don't do everything perfectly. The result was that I had lost perspective on, well, everything. My parenting compass was like a GPS that was constantly rerouting, sending me off in a million different directions, none of which seemed to take me where I wanted to go. Week after week, my therapist and I sorted through all of the parenting advice and suggestions and worries and what-ifs, and we laid it all out there as if we were on some reality hoarding show. I walked out with a few useful thoughts to carry me through the week, imagining the rest of it spread out on a blue tarp on the floor of her office, with a big TOSS sign next to it.

★ **I learned skills and strategies for managing my triggers and tough moments.** These were often small changes that made a big difference. For example, when my girls were toddlers, I had a friend

PUBLIC SERVICE ANNOUNCEMENT

MEDICATION WAS HELPFUL to me, but please don't drop this book and rush off to your doctor for a prescription. I've said it before, and I'll say it again. There is no magic pill or secret shortcut or twenty-seven-step program for only $19.95 that will help you stop losing your shit with your kids and turn you into a Perfect Parent overnight. Such a thing does not exist, so stop looking for it. Medication was just one piece that helped me put my puzzle back together. Sleep was crucial, as were exercise, self-care, and the support of my therapist and family.

myself. I stayed on the meds for about a year before tapering off with the help of my prescriber.

Which brings us to where I am now. I sleep through the night most of the time, I've lost much of the weight I gained, and I'm not on any medications. I still get triggered, but I'm more aware of my triggers and the ways in which they make it more likely that I will lose my temper. I know that I need to sleep and exercise and keep a snack in my purse and slow down and talk to my friends and laugh my ass off on a regular basis, and I know that these behaviors aren't self-indulgences but *absolute requirements* if I want to be with my kids without lashing out at the them. I also know that parenting is hard and there will always be days I don't stick to my plan, or I do but shit happens anyway, and I still lose it. When I do explode, I'm much more likely to take a few deep breaths, do a silly dance, apologize to my kids, and have a whole lot more compassion for all of us.

Perhaps most importantly, I no longer believe that losing my shit is a moral failing or that I should be able to simply *choose* to stay calm. I see my explosions as a symptom, a red flag letting me know that I need to take care of myself, or get some support, or just accept defeat for the day and turn on the TV (which I no longer see as a failure). And I have the skills and strategies to get back on track.

That's my story. Now it's your turn. The details of your personal and parenting challenges might look similar to mine, or they may be completely different. Either way, there are a couple of aspects of my experience that are fairly common. First, it took me a long time to realize how much I was struggling. I was so deep in the weeds of work and life and raising children that not only could I not see the forest for the trees, but I kept tripping over the damn roots and thinking it was all my fault. It wasn't, and it's not your fault either. If you're years into your parenting journey and still having a hard time, it's OK. It's never too late to turn things around.

The other life-changing lesson I learned is that I couldn't—and can't—do any of it alone. I am immensely grateful to my village: the family members, friends, experts, and professionals who have supported me for years and continue to do so. They held my babies, listened to my worries, taught me what was typical and when to take action, suggested I get help (Hi, hubby, I love you, even if I never listen to you!) and stuck with me through it all.

In addition to providing information and advice, I hope this book is a source of support, a reminder that I'm part of your village, even if we never meet. I hope my story empowers you to reach out to others, but in the meantime, I'm here. I'll walk you through each step of the getting-your-shit-together process. The first step is getting a handle on your triggers, so let's get to it.

CHAPTER 3

Know Thy Shit: Owning Your Buttons and Triggers

YOUR TRIGGERS ARE MAKING YOU CRAZY

★

HOW TO KNOW WHEN YOU'RE TRIGGERED

★

WHAT'S SETTING YOU OFF?

We all have triggers. They're just part of the deal. In the event that you're tempted to skip over this chapter because you think you don't have any issues, well, don't do that. This information matters, so grab your coffee and get comfortable.

For the purposes of this book, a trigger is *anything that makes it more likely that you will lose your shit with your kids*. It does this by making your buttons bigger, brighter, and more sensitive to pushing.

While it's true that anyone, from your cousins to your colleagues, can push your buttons and cause you to lose your shit, this book is about losing your shit with your kids, so we're going to focus on them. Children, by definition, are professional button pushers. They move through the world with their fingers out, ready to touch and push everything that crosses their path. This is part of how kids learn, grow, and interact with the world. Unfortunately, they often do this in inconsistent, unpredictable, and problematic ways. It just goes with the territory of having a partially developed kid brain.

When you're not triggered, your kid's behavior is less likely to push your buttons, because your buttons aren't readily available. I'm talking about those glorious moments when you're somehow able to stay patient and kind in the face of your child's antics.

When you *are* triggered, however, it's a different story. Your nervous system is on high alert, ready to send you into either Fight, Flight,

Freeze, or Freak Out, at the push of a button. Your buttons light up and migrate to a spot right at eye level for your kiddo, not unlike that damn emergency button in the elevator. (WHY DO THEY PUT THEM THERE? That was a rhetorical question. I know why.)

Children, by definition, are professional button pushers.

Which brings us back to your kid, wandering around, finger out, looking for action. And then they find a button. You bet your tushy they're going to push the crap out of it. The younger, more immature, more exhausted, or more triggered your kids are, the harder and faster they're going to shove their grubby little fingers right into your weak spots.

Maybe you can handle one push of the button, or even two or twelve, depending on whether or not your lower back is acting up, how far behind you are on your bills, and how cranky your boss was at work. Eventually, though, even the most chill among us will lose it, and we need to understand why. This is some next-level adulting we're about to do here, folks. We're going to own our shit, by which I mean identify our triggers and figure out how to deal with them so our buttons become smaller, dimmer, less sensitive, and ultimately less pushable.

Notice what I said there. I said we're going to make those buttons *less* pushable. I did *not* say that we're going to keep our kids from pushing them. This is a crucially important distinction because when we focus on how our kids are pushing our buttons, the implied fix is to get them to stop doing whatever it is that they're doing. While it's technically true that kids can be both triggers and pushers, focusing on them as triggers is a no-go for two reasons:

1. As I've said before, hinging our sanity and functioning on some-one else's insane behavior is a losing proposition. You cannot hold other people responsible for what you do or don't do, especially when those other people happen to be your offspring. The reality is that kids will always do stupid shit, and they will always push your buttons. You're unlikely to change that. Your job is to take care of your buttons as much as you can and to stay as calm as possible when your kids get to them.

BUT I STILL NEED TO KNOW HOW TO DEAL WITH MY KID!

AT THIS POINT, you might be thinking that it's all fine and good to focus on your triggers and buttons, but your kid is also a major part of the picture. Perhaps you have a child whose behavior is challenging or confusing to you, or maybe she's in a developmental stage that you just don't know how to manage. You suspect there are more skillful ways to parent, but you don't know what they are. Here are a few thoughts for you:

Your number one job as a parent is to keep your kid safe. Do the best you can.

Your number two job is to manage your emotions so you can respond to your children intentionally and without losing your shit. That's what this book is all about.

From there, you need to figure out how you want to raise your children, which is as much about how you respond to them as anything. There are as many right ways to do this as there are parents out there; the trick is to find what works for you and your family. Having a plan for how you're going to respond when your kiddo smacks his brother or lies to your face or loses yet another retainer will help you stay calm in tricky moments. Here are a few ways to find your plan:

★ Start with the people who actually know you and your kids. These may include members of your family, your friends, or the doctors who care for you

2. **It's not developmentally appropriate to expect children to behave well all the time.** This is especially true if they're triggered or struggling with developmental, emotional, physical, or intellectual challenges or if it's a Tuesday or their moon is in Mercury. Their prefrontal cortex, the part of their brain that is responsible for keeping them in line, literally doesn't exist yet. It's like asking them to build a house without any wood or tools. It ain't gonna happen.

all. Share your concerns and ask for their advice.

★ Look to your culture and community for ideas and practices. This may include your religious or spiritual community, fellow parents, or teachers and counselors at your child's school.

★ Talk to an expert, such as a family therapist, child psychologist, or parent coach.

★ Seek advice from parenting books, webinars, or podcasts. Just remember to keep a little perspective as you take in the advice. Does it seem like a good fit for the structure, style, and values of your family? If not, keep looking.

★ Remember there are many excellent ways to parent. Be wary of anyone who encourages you to believe that their way is the only one.

★ Even if you have a plan, you're not going to make the right choice every time. You will get it wrong, and that's OK. The good news is that whatever you come up with from a place of calm attention will be better than what you bust out with when you're pissed and frustrated. Do your best and hang in there; your kids will give you another opportunity to try again soon.

★ Finally, remember that it's not your job to keep your kids happy. Big emotions don't need to be *fixed*, they need to be *felt*. Children need to learn that there's nothing wrong with feeling sad or mad or embarrassed or confused and that eventually those feelings will pass. If you can't tolerate their meltdowns, they won't be able to either. It all starts with you, so saddle up and get ready.

To be absolutely clear, I'm not suggesting you give up all hope and let the kids go feral. Of course you need to set limits, hold boundaries, maintain expectations, and teach them about appropriate behavior and self-awareness and indoor voices, but you're not doing it so they'll stop triggering you. You're doing it so someday they'll be functional members of society. These are long-term skills that many adults still haven't mastered. I don't know about you, but I don't want to spend the next several years losing my shit while I wait for my kids to stop pushing my buttons.

> I'm not suggesting you give up all hope and let the kids go feral.

Even as we continue to teach our kids how to wait their turn and wash their hands, we also need to accept that we can't control every aspect of their behavior. This realization frees us up to focus on what we *can* control—our own triggers and buttons. We're gonna go straight-up Serenity Prayer on ourselves; deal with our triggers when we can, accept the ones we can't, and get damn good at recognizing the difference. The first step, the one we're going to explore in this chapter, is identifying our triggers. Many of us walk around lit up, freaked out, or pissed off to some degree or another, without even realizing (a) that it's happening or (b) that it makes it much more likely that we're going to lose our shit. It doesn't matter if the trigger has nothing to do with your kids. You're just one person, with one set of buttons, and regardless of what gets them going, they're still there, just waiting for your kid to push them.

Everything You Need to Know About Your Triggers and Buttons

. . . . • . . . . • • . . . . . . ••

First, there are a few things you need to know about triggers and buttons:

★ **Triggers can be universal or unique.** Universal triggers, such as exhaustion, chronic pain, or grief, tend to put everyone on edge, regardless of personal differences. Unique triggers, however, impact some folks but not others. For example, loud noise (including live music, whether it's coming from my kids or my favorite band) makes me tense and cranky, whereas my husband seems totally immune to it. Parenting is easier when loud noises don't bother you, so yay for him and boo for me. There's not much I can do about this other than (a) accept that this is a thing for me, (b) get intermittently annoyed at my husband because it doesn't bother him one bit, and (c) try to minimize the noise in my life whenever I can. Earplugs, anyone?

★ **Triggers can be chronic or acute.** Some of them, such as a sprained ankle or stressful work project, have an end in sight. We may live with other triggers, such as a permanent disability or a trauma history, for our entire lives. When this happens, our buttons may always be a bit bigger or more sensitive than they might have otherwise been.

★ **The more frequently your buttons are triggered and pushed, the more quickly and easily they will be pushed in the future.** This is basic neurobiology; neurons that fire together, wire together. Learning an instrument is a great example; as your child practices reading the music and playing each note, her brain eventually gets so good at coordinating what she sees with her eyes and does with her hands that she can play an entire song without consciously thinking about how to move each finger. The same is true for triggers and buttons and shit loss, which is both totally annoying and fairly hopeful. Just as we can "get better" at freaking out, we can also get better at cooling down; the more we practice, the faster, more naturally, and more easily we'll be able to respond calmly.

★ **Some triggers are about just you, and some aren't.** They may involve other people, including your family, friends, colleagues, neighbors, or the parents you see every day at pickup. Other triggers might be entirely based on whatever is happening in your mind or body at any given moment.

★ **You may have some amount of control over some triggers but very little or no control over others.** For example, I could choose not to answer my friend's frantic phone calls each night, but there's nothing I can do about the wailing siren of an ambulance that puts me on edge every time I hear it. The goal is to know the difference and work from there.

★ **Triggers change over time.** Dynamics and issues and people that used to get you going might not even register on your radar anymore, while other challenges and concerns will come out of the woodwork and light you up like a Christmas tree. Some of these changes are fairly predictable, while others just aren't. For example, if feeding an infant is particularly stressful for you, hang in there. He'll be feeding himself in a few months. Alternately, you may find that the constant physical contact of parenting means that touch is now a trigger for you, even if it wasn't before.

★ **Positive experiences can also be triggers.** Sometimes a seemingly joyful experience (like having a baby or getting a promotion) can light up your buttons for a variety of reasons, such as the pressure of increased expectations, shifting relationships, fear of failure, or just the mere fact that any sort of change can be stressful.

★ **Your coping skills might actually be triggering you or activating other triggers.** In my case, I tried to manage my anxiety and boost my energy with chocolate and coffee, but any short-term relief I experienced was obliterated by the long-term consequences of weight gain and chronic exhaustion. Many parents respond to uncomfortable feelings and experiences by picking up their smartphones or wineglasses, both of which run the risk of lighting up their buttons even as they're trying to calm them down.

★ **Parenting can be a trigger.** Raising children will reveal vulnerabilities and buttons you didn't even know you had, often related to your childhood. You're back in a parent-child relationship for the first time since you were a kid, and even though you're the grown-up this time around, your brain and body don't always remember that. So, if your parents yelled at you every time you upended your Cheerios, messy accidents may be a trigger for you even if you weren't previously one to cry over spilled milk.

Your Tells
HOW TO KNOW IF YOU'RE TRIGGERED

· ·

I t's entirely possible that you're triggered to some degree or another at some point or another every single day, and you have no freaking clue. Your nervous system didn't evolve for insight; it evolved for survival. Your limbic system doesn't give a hoot if you realize you're freaking out; it's just trying to keep you alive. This is why our brains respond to stress reflexively—by speeding up our hearts, tensing our muscles, and dilating our pupils—rather than diverting resources and energy to our prefrontal cortex, which might enable us to notice when we're triggered, calm ourselves down, and think clearly.

Fortunately, you can get better at noticing when our buttons have gotten especially sensitive and pushable, which is the crucial first step toward cooling them down. It's all about your *tells*: the thoughts, feelings, bodily sensations, and behaviors that show up whenever you're triggered. Within those four categories, everyone has different tells, so it's important for you to recognize your own. (More thoughts on this in Chapter 8.)

Here are a few common tells:

★ Anxious, obsessive, or "stuck" thinking or worrying

★ Physical tension, such as a tight back, furrowed brow, or hunched shoulders

★ Fantasies of going all Thelma & Louise on the situation, which could range from launching yourself off a cliff to just disappearing into the aisles of Target for a few hours

★ Feeling irritable or easily annoyed

★ Nitpicking and micromanaging your children, spouse, or any unfortunate soul who has had the bad luck to cross your path at that particular moment (This can include sending naggy or rude texts, tweets, or emails.)

YOU CAN'T EAT, DRINK, OR SPEND YOUR WAY OUT OF TRIGGERS

DRINKING, USING DRUGS, gambling, gaming, compulsive eating, watching pornography, or spending yourself into debt are all-too-common responses to the experience of being triggered. Unfortunately, they don't work. They might distract you or dull your senses for a few hours, but at the end of the day, you haven't actually dealt with the trigger or taken care of yourself. Dig yourself too deep into your hole of choice and you'll end up addicted.

If you're struggling with any of these issues, keep reading. The strategies in the following chapters will teach you how to respond skillfully to difficult triggers. However, if you are dealing with an addiction, they may not be enough. Your challenges aren't a moral failing, and they don't mean you're a bad parent or terrible person. You're just up against something much bigger than yourself. Finding the time, money, resources, or childcare to get help may feel impossible, but it also may be the most important choice you ever make for yourself, your children, and your family. Reach out to a friend, your doctor, a therapist, a clergy member, or support group. Healing and change aren't easy, but they are possible and most definitely worth it.

★ Making snarky comments under your breath or rolling your eyes

★ Craving sugar, snacks, alcohol, nicotine, or other drugs

★ Picking at your skin or scabs or biting your nails (Grown-ups do this too!)

★ Reaching for your smartphone or repeatedly checking social media

★ Stressing about getting things done *NOW* (For me, it's the dishwasher. When I'm triggered, a dishwasher that needs to be unloaded becomes a code-red emergency.)

★ Rushing unnecessarily

★ And, of course, losing your shit with your kids

The Most Common Triggers

We're ready to explore what some of your triggers might be. (There's also a ridiculously long list at the end of this book, in case you need additional help identifying yours.) The goal is to figure out what is lighting up your buttons and making them super pushable so you can take effective steps to calm yourself down, both preemptively and in response to difficult moments. Here are some of the most common triggers among the parents I know and work with:

CHRONIC EXHAUSTION. Even if you are getting eight hours of shut-eye each night, you might not be getting high-quality sleep. In addition, chronic stress, busyness, and overwhelm will leave you feeling depleted by the end of the day.

MULTITASKING WHILE YOU'RE WITH YOUR KIDS. The idea that any of us can do more than one thing at a time is a myth; if even one of those things involves your kids, well, forget it. Trying to do too much at once increases stress levels unnecessarily. (This is such a significant and underappreciated trigger that I've devoted all of Chapter 4 to it.)

ANXIETY, which may include worried thoughts that you have a hard time managing, feeling keyed up or restless, difficulty focusing or concentrating, irritability, tense muscles, being easily fatigued, and difficulty falling or staying asleep.

YOUR SMARTPHONE, including being constantly connected and available, the insanity of social media, and the insidious notifications distracting the hell out of you all the time.

MAJOR LIFE CHANGES, including death, divorce, moving, job loss, or illness or injury. These are the times in our lives when we most need to ramp up our self-care, and yet they're also when we're least likely to do so. Oh, the irony.

CHRONIC STRESS. As we'll discuss later, I think of stress as the thought, belief, or perception that you can't handle what's going on, whatever that may be. Whether or not your perception is accurate, stress is a significant trigger for pretty much everyone.

GAMES AND ACTIVITIES AS TRIGGERS

IT'S PRETTY EASY to notice the worst triggers, such as major illnesses or accidents. But even seemingly benign experiences can trigger us. Example: your kid's soccer game. If you love watching your kids play and chatting with the other parents, that's awesome. But games can be giant triggerfests for many parents. The hot sun, the stress of not knowing anyone else, the social pressure to look good and say something moderately entertaining, the worry about whether your kid sucks at organized sports, the boredom, and the subsequent desire to check your phone (not to mention the guilt you feel each time you do)—it doesn't take much to turn an innocent soccer field into a potential minefield.

Fortunately, you can do something about it. Step one is owning that you don't love soccer or soccer-related activities. This doesn't mean you're a bad parent or you don't love your child; it just means you don't love soccer. That's all. Don't make it into something bigger than it is.

Next, decide what you're going to do. If you feel compelled to go to the damn game, then anticipate the triggers and deal with them. Eat a big breakfast and bring snacks and a water bottle. Wear a hat. Bring a chair and a book. Walk laps around the field. Stick your headphones in your ears and turn on a good audiobook or podcast. Stop stressing about what everyone else thinks. (That last one is not easy, but it will get easier, and you will feel like a major badass once you master it. Try to remember that you're not a negligent parent; just the opposite. You're taking care of yourself so you don't lose your shit.)

There is one other option: Don't go to the game. Send your partner or grandparent or ask a fellow parent to drop your child off or pick them up. There are many ways to show up for your kid and you don't have to do all of them. Ditch the ones that trigger you and you'll have more time and energy for the ones that don't. (And if it isn't immediately clear to you, this doesn't just apply to soccer. If you're triggered by robotics tournaments, clarinet lessons, or Model UN, then bring your headphones, take a walk outside, or organize a carpool. Just do whatever it takes to remove this trigger from your life.)

GREAT. THANKS A LOT.
What Exactly Am I Supposed to Do Now?

O ne of my social-work mentors likes to remind me that insight is the booby prize—the award given as a joke to the person who finishes last or totally blows the race altogether. This will make sense to those of you who are wondering what the hell you're supposed to do now.

You don't have to fix your triggers or eliminate them altogether. Rather, I want you to focus on Awareness, Acceptance, and Action.

Awareness is about recognizing when you're at risk of being triggered or that you are already triggered. When you can notice your tells (such as holding your breath or giving your kids the finger when they're not looking) and see them as helpful warning signs rather than irrelevant irritations, you're giving yourself a chance to deal with them before you explode. We'll talk a lot more about the skill of noticing—why it's so powerful and how to get better at it—in Chapter 8.

The next step involves *accepting* that you're triggered. It can be tempting to try to ignore what's going on or push through it, but such responses virtually never work. Your nervous system doesn't give a crap if this is an inconvenient time for a freak-out, and the more you fight against it, the more triggered you'll become. But let me be very clear: Acceptance isn't about lying down and letting your triggers steamroll you. It's just about acknowledging the reality of your life. So

> Wouldn't it be great if we could make all of our triggers just go away? Yeah, well, we're not in Kansas anymore, Toto.

if your current response to this chapter is any version of squeezing your eyes shut, sticking your fingers in your ears, and singing LALALALALALALALALA at the top of your lungs, well, maybe it's time to try something else. If texting with your brother is a trigger for you, own it and figure out what you're going to do about it. You're a grown-up now, you can do this.

OK, so you did the awareness and acceptance pieces (oh, if only it were that easy). You're ready for *action*. Here are your options: Fix it or learn to live with it.

Let's start with fix it, because that's the best one. Wouldn't it be great if we could make all of our triggers just go away? Yeah, well, we're not in Kansas anymore, Toto. Lasting fixes are few and far between, so if one is available to you, JUMP ON IT. If you can quit that miserable job or wear noise-canceling headphones on the train or resign from that committee or finally lay the smackdown with your parents around their surprise visits or get your tushy to physical therapy to deal with your shoulder, well, freaking do it already.

And if you can't fix your triggers, then you need to learn to live with them.

We'll talk more about what it means to live with your triggers in upcoming chapters, but first, here's an example from my life: On a recent vacation, my family and I were at a small restaurant, waiting to be seated for breakfast. It was just one room, lit up with bright fluorescent lights and crammed with people. It was noisy and loud and people kept bumping into me as they made their way to their seats or out the door. I was hungry and I hadn't slept well in the hotel room the night before. Trigger. Trigger. Trigger. I was one giant red button, and my kids were pushing the crap out of it. They were talking too loudly, pointing at people, hanging on my arms, stepping on my feet, and asking a million insane and irrelevant questions.

I had been working on this book, so I was actually aware that I was getting triggered. I'd also been talking to my husband about it, so he was thinking about it too. He saw that I was teetering, so the minute we were able to sit down, he put me in the seat nearest the wall (where I was least likely to be jostled or bumped) and told the girls to leave me alone until the food came.

Normally I would get all pissy and cranky, and I'd probably snap at him to stop bossing me around and telling me where to sit and generally treating me like I was mentally unstable (even though I was absolutely unstable at that particular moment). But I was *aware* and able to *accept* that I was about to lose it, so I took his advice and sat in the corner. My husband proceeded to entertain the girls, so I could stare quietly into my coffee and breathe. Once the meal was over, we decided to walk back to the hotel instead of taking a cab because I know that being outside and moving my body are two of my most effective strategies for cooling down my overheated system. These *actions*—breathing, eating, getting outside, and walking—helped me get about as calm as a parent on vacation with two young kids can get. While there is no fix for the ways in which sensory stimulation triggers me, I am learning to live with it.

> I was one giant red button, and my kids were pushing the crap out of it.

The bad news is that triggers are a major bummer. The other bad news is that they're an unavoidable reality of life. The good news is that you can learn to deal with your triggers skillfully by avoiding them when you can and doing your best to minimize their impact when you can't. While this will require some learning and habit-changing on your part, it's all pretty simple and straightforward, and the more you practice the easier it will get. There are a variety of ways to reduce and manage the triggers in your life, and we're going to explore many of them in depth over the next four chapters.

How Doing Less Will Help You Not Lose Your Shit

SELF-CARE FOR PEOPLE WHO DESPISE SELF-CARE

★

MULTITASKING: NOT AS AWESOME AS YOU'D LIKE TO THINK

★

YOUR PHONE IS MAKING YOU LOSE YOUR SHIT

Over the next four chapters, we're going to explore eleven different practices that will cool down your nervous system, keep your brain clear and functional (or at least as clear and functional as your foggy parent brain is capable of getting), and dramatically decrease the likelihood that you will explode at your kids. I realize this is a lot to dump on a busy parent's plate, so for the sake of your sanity, we'll start with four nonnegotiables: single-tasking, sleep, support, and self-compassion.

These may look suspiciously like self-care, I know. If self-care isn't your gig, or feels super indulgent, remember this: You're not doing this for yourself, or at least not only for yourself. You're doing it for your children, your relationship with them, and a calmer family dynamic overall. You're also doing it to feel less like a crazy person who

> If self-care isn't your gig, or feels super indulgent, remember this: You're not doing this for yourself, or at least not only for yourself.

keeps exploding all over the place. You can also think of all of this as Shit You *Have* to Do So You Won't Lose Your Shit with Your Kids, if that helps you feel better about doing it.

As apt as it may be, the phrase "shit you have to do so you won't lose your shit" is fairly unwieldy (and makes for a terrible acronym), so we'll call these eleven practices your **BuRPs**: **B**utton **R**eduction **P**ractices. I've chosen these BuRPs because they're free, simple, evidence-based, and specifically designed to reduce the size and sensitivity of your buttons.

Having said that, these changes will take time and energy on your part. Hey, if getting your shit together were quick and easy, you would have done it by now, right? The good news is that you'll have more time and energy when you're not spending so much of it blowing up at your kids. The other good news is that you'll be less likely to drop, lose, break, or forget things, or say, email, or tweet things you don't mean. Basically, you'll spend less of your life cleaning up unnecessary messes. Oh, and you'll probably be healthier and your mood will improve too.

BuRPS LOCATOR

HERE'S A COMPLETE list of all the BuRPs in this book and the chapters where you can find them.

CHAPTER 4
Single-Tasking

CHAPTER 5
Sleep • Support • Self-Compassion

CHAPTER 6
Simplify • Stretch • Seek Silence • Slow Down • Say Thank You • Breathe

CHAPTER 7
Space from Your Kids

How to Rock Your BuRPs

. . . .

As you jump into these life changes, please don't worry about whether you've bought the right clothes or gadgets (totally unnecessary) or if you're practicing the "right" or the "wrong" way or doing everything perfectly or not. That kind of black-or-white thinking is a setup for failure, so try to let it go. Instead, consider these two questions as you figure out how to integrate each practice into your busy life:

IS IT *WORKABLE*? Can you actually do the thing I'm asking you to do? If not, can you tweak the practice so it will work for you? Or can you find something else that will work better? These Button Reduction Practices are designed to be workable for anyone, so if you're really honestly, absolutely convinced that you can't move your body more or take a break from your phone for an hour every night, then you may have a lifestyle that is inherently incompatible with not losing your shit at your kids. Please note that I did *not* say that you are inherently incapable of not losing your shit. I said your lifestyle isn't a match for staying calm in the face of your little button pushers. I hope you can see the difference.

> Black-or-white thinking is a setup for failure, so try to let it go.

WHEN YOUR LIFE IS INCOMPATIBLE WITH NOT LOSING YOUR SHIT

I JUST SAID THAT if you have found it absolutely impossible to make time in your daily life to sleep, move your body, and slow down, for example, then you may have a lifestyle that is inherently incompatible with not losing your shit with your kids. This is a bold statement, I know, but it's also true. Remember, it's not about you; it's about the context in which you are parenting. I have worked with many parents who have struggled with this very issue, and it's a tough situation. Having said that, change is possible. It's not easy, and it can take time and a lot of support to figure out, but it is possible.

Here are a few examples of the significant life changes my friends and clients have made in response to the challenges of life and parenting:

★ Stepping down from most, if not all, volunteer opportunities or optional obligations

★ Cutting way back on the children's activities, such as sports, music lessons, or other after-school clubs or groups

★ Reaching out to friends and family for more support in intentional, consistent ways, including setting up regular childcare swaps and carpools whenever possible

★ Shifting from full-time to part-time work

★ Leaving a job entirely (at least for now)

★ Hiring a nanny, au pair, or regular babysitter or parent's helper

Contemplating such changes can feel overwhelming, if not impossible. It may help to remember that these changes don't have to be permanent. Give yourself and your family the time you need to settle down, calm down, and get things back on track, and then you can reevaluate.

IS IT WORKING? Is the practice helping you lose your shit with your kids less often? If so, that's great! If it's not, then consider whether (a) you're actually doing the thing you allege to be doing and (b) if you've given it enough time to start working. If the answer to either of these questions is no, that's OK. You can always start again. Rome wasn't built in a day, and you won't get your shit together in a day either. However, if you've given these practices a serious try for at least a few weeks and you're still epically losing it, then you need to try something else. Review your triggers and try to notice any patterns in the what, when, where, and why of your explosions. That might give you a little clarity about what to try next.

A few more notes on BuRPs:

★ I'm using the word *practice* in a very specific, intentional way, and I'm not talking about a job (like a dental or law practice) or something you *think* about doing occasionally. You know what I mean. Putting on your gym clothes and then sitting on the couch checking email instead of actually exercising, well, that ain't practicing. You gotta get off the couch.

★ In addition, these practices are *dose dependent*, which is just a fancy-pants way of saying that the more you do it, the more you'll experience the benefits. I'm not saying you should sleep fifteen hours a day (though doesn't that sound nice?). It's all about balance. But the more consistently you stretch, slow down, or breathe, the better you'll get at staying cool when life heats up.

★ Speaking of doses, the more you're struggling, the more you need your BuRPs. When you're down with the flu, you need more rest than usual. When your anxiety spikes, try to do just one thing at a time, get some extra support, and move your body. Having said all of that, please don't wait until the shit hits the fan to start practicing. It's hard enough to develop new habits; don't make it any harder by waiting until you're at your worst to start something new.

★ Finally, you need to practice your BuRPs regularly. What you do every day is more important than what you do every once in a while. So don't come at me with the baloney my daughter pulled when she told me she didn't need to pee on the potty ever again because she'd done that once already, thankyouverymuch. Stick with your BuRPs as consistently as you can, and don't give up when you fall off the wagon. Just dust yourself off and get back on.

★ Consider your major triggers, and start with the practices that are most likely to address them. If you're always exhausted, focus on sleep. If you're constantly feeling overwhelmed or always losing your keys, try simplifying and single-tasking.

This stuff isn't rocket science, and it doesn't have to be a huge deal. I'm not asking you to go vegan or become a hot-yoga devotee (unless that works for you—then go for it). These are small, simple practices that require no fancy equipment and are almost all free. Think about it this way: You don't need to be an A+ parent. Aim

> You don't need to be an A+ parent. Aim for a solid B: If you can remember your BuRPs about 80 percent of the time, that's awesome.

for a solid B: If you can remember your BuRPs about 80 percent of the time, that's awesome. If we let kids drop out of school every time they didn't ace an exam, our children would be totally uneducated, and even worse, we'd be stuck at home with them all day. The reason we keep sending them back to class is the same reason you need to stick with this stuff, even when it's hard. With more practice, your kids will get better at taking tests and you'll get better at not losing your shit.

There are four main practices: Single-tasking, Sleep, Support, and Self-compassion. (Yes, they all start with S, and yes, I am extremely clever. Thank you for noticing.) Basically, *the goal is to do one thing at a time during the day, one thing at night (get some zzzzs), get as much help with all of it as you can, and cut yourself serious slack when it falls apart anyway.* These four BuRPs are nonnegotiable. And the ability to focus on just one thing at a time is such a powerful strategy for keeping your shit together that we're going to spend the rest of this chapter on it.

How My Husband Taught Me to Ignore the Dishes

. . . .

66 "I am exhausted. I am done. D.O.N.E. DONE. Get these kids away from me while I soak in the bathtub and stare at the wall." Those are the words I greeted my husband with each time I handed off

the girls after I'd been alone with them for an extended period of time. No matter how well or poorly behaved they were, parenting wore me out, stressed me out, and left me at high risk of losing my shit.

My husband, on the other hand, never seemed quite so overwhelmed after a day with the girls. I'd ask him how it went, he'd say "fine," and he meant it. It's not that our kids were always angelic for him, but somehow their unpredictability and neediness didn't bother him the same way it triggered me.

Over time, I got curious about this difference. What was his secret (other than being an innately more stable human being than I am)? That was right around the time I started learning about and practicing mindfulness, which is all about noticing. And one of the first things I noticed each time I got home from my mindfulness class was that the house was a freaking mess. I didn't have to ask what my husband and the girls did while I was out; the toys scattered across the living room told me they had played Memory and worked on a puzzle, the dirty dishes on the counter revealed what they had for dinner, and I knew the Berenstain Bears books were in heavy rotation, as they were still scattered across the couch.

My immediate reaction to the messy house was a mix of exasperation, frustration, and utter defeat. Mostly, I was pissed. I never left the house that way when I was alone with the girls. My husband almost always came home to clean counters, a gently humming dishwasher, and a tidy living room. Why the hell couldn't he extend me the same courtesy?

We had several fights about this before I realized that the state of the house and the state of my sanity were related, but not in the way I had assumed. Clutter is a major trigger for me (although I wasn't aware of the connection at the time), so I was constantly cleaning and tidying while I was with the girls. I would pick a card in Candy Land, move my cardboard character, and fold a few towels before my next turn, all the while silently cursing the inventor of that mind-numbing game. I'd read a picture book out loud while mentally reviewing my task list, negotiate squabbles while chopping cucumbers, or text my friends while swaddling stuffed animals in blankets fashioned from kitchen towels. Instead of sitting with the girls at meals, I would take the opportunity to empty the dishwasher or write out a shopping list.

Multitasking isn't really a thing. It's just a word we silly humans use to delude ourselves into thinking we can do several different things at once.

I was constantly in motion and frequently stressed, primarily because I was trying to accomplish more than one thing at a time. My husband was doing nothing of the sort. When he was with the girls, he was just with them. On the one hand, the house was a mess at the end of the day, but on the other, he wasn't a twitchy ball of nerves, a bright red button just waiting to be pushed. The difference was that I was constantly multitasking and he wasn't.

Once I realized all of this, I began to change my ways (without ever admitting any of it to my husband, of course). The dishes now sit dirty in the sink until the end of the day. The toys cover the floor, and the markers stay on the kitchen table until the girls do one final pre-bedtime cleanup. (If the clutter gets on my nerves before the end of the day, we pause whatever we're doing and take a moment to tidy.) Either way, it rarely takes more than twenty minutes to clean up, and I'm a hell of a lot less grumpy both during and afterward. Now, whenever I find myself getting tense or stressed with the girls, the first thing I do is notice whether I'm multitasking. If I am, I call a time-out on my brain and try to focus on whatever is right in front of me, which inevitably calms me down.

Multitasking Is a Myth

H opefully, you know by now that multitasking isn't really a thing. It's just a word we silly humans use to delude ourselves into thinking we can do several different things at once. Sadly, we can't. But we refuse to let go of the dream, so instead we yank our attention from the boiling noodles to the spelling words to the buzzing phone while snapping at a kid to flush the toilet. Unfortunately, our bodies and awareness can't quite keep up with all of the task switching (as it's officially called), which is why we end up spilling the noodles and misspelling the words and the damn toilet never gets flushed after all, the end result of which is a colossal and totally unnecessary stress explosion.

Speaking of which, this is a good time to talk about stress. It's a word we throw around frequently, often without a clear sense of what it means. As I mentioned before, here's the definition I like: *Stress is the belief, feeling, or thought that we cannot handle whatever is happening.* It doesn't matter if it's a feverish child, a fender bender, or a load of wet laundry that should have been transferred to the dryer last night; if you believe for any reason that you do not have the skills or resources to deal with the situation, you're going to feel stressed out.

> Multitasking is a surefire way to trick yourself into believing you can't handle what's going on.

Sometimes your perception will be spot on: You can't handle it, and you need to get support, help, or advice. But there are plenty of times when you're stressing about a situation that you are totally capable of managing. Either way, if you think you're in over your head, your nervous system is going to put itself on red alert, which puts you at high risk of losing it with your kids.

Multitasking is a surefire way to trick yourself into believing you can't handle what's going on. The more balls you have in the air, the more likely you are to drop one, right? Of course, there will be times when you have little or no control over how many balls come flying at you, in which case you can either find someone to help catch some of them, or you can accept that some of them are going to fall, or you can keep your head down until the circus finally ends. But you'd be surprised by how many balls you can choose to set down, even for two or ten minutes at a time, and how much less stressed you feel when you have only one ball to keep your eye on.

Research has also found that multitasking increases our stress indirectly in the following ways:

★ **It makes us more distracted and less attentive**, making it way more likely that we'll spill the blueberries, lose the permission slip, or forget to buckle the baby's car-seat straps.

★ **It increases our anxiety and dampens our creativity**, which means we worry more than we need to and have a harder time thinking up effective solutions and responses.

★ **It makes it more likely we'll miss important information and cues.** If we had just noticed that the kids were getting hungry or overtired, we could have given them a snack or a nap before they freaked out.

★ **It makes us less efficient** because we're only half-doing whatever it is we think we're doing, which means it will take twice as long to finish it, and that's assuming we don't screw anything up along the way.

Multitasking is pervasive and insidious, especially when we're totally unaware that we're even doing it. It is absolutely one of the most common and underappreciated causes of parental shit loss. Trying to do more than one thing at a time is inherently triggering. Multitasking tricks us into thinking we're being all productive and adulty and awesome when we're actually hurling ourselves headlong into a meltdown. Now, as we dig into this, please don't freak out. I'm not suggesting that you need to turn yourself into a hyper-focused, slow-motion, monk-style parent. Remember, we're not going for perfection. I'm just asking you to remember that multitasking is a trigger that you have more control over than you may have previously realized.

MULTITASKING ISN'T JUST ABOUT WHAT YOU'RE *DOING*

TO ADD TO the chaos, multi-tasking isn't just about doing more than one thing at a time; it can be about thinking more than one thought at a time. This sort of multi-thinking, as we can call it, is especially problematic if your thoughts are only tangentially related (if at all) to the task at hand.

Let's say, for example, that you want your child to learn to ride a bike, but said child is anxious about riding without training wheels and consistently resists your instructions and suggestions. And, if in addition to monitoring the street for cars and guiding your nervous rider, you're also noticing how all the other kids on the block are zooming around, while also picturing how colossally screwed up your kid's life will be if they never learn to ride a bicycle, well, that might stress you out.

Judging, comparing, stressing, worrying, or fantasizing about who

your child is or isn't, what they may or may not accomplish someday, or where they are or aren't developmentally is an insidious method of multitasking and an all-too-common cause of shit loss. And before you know it, you're snapping at your child, thereby increasing their anxiety, which makes the whole bike-riding experience way more stressful than it needs to be.

The alternative is to notice your exploding thoughts and do what you can to focus your thinking (more on this in Chapter 6). Pay attention to your child; be cool with who your kid is right now and what they can do right now. If you can't do that, get someone else to teach them how to ride a bike. That's a totally legit option. Either way, as soon as you realize that your mind is doing one thing and your body is doing something else, do what you can to get them back on the same track.

How to Stop Multitasking

· ·

Let me be clear: I'm not saying that you should set a goal of never, ever doing more than one thing a time. That's impossible, so go ahead and stick it in your Perfect Shit That Ain't Gonna Happen file and lock it away. I just want you to start noticing how multitasking may be connected to your loss of shit and to see single-tasking as one of the many strategies you can employ when you need to cool your buttons down.

Single-tasking is the practice of doing just one thing at a time, and it is *awesome*. Getting your mind and body focused on the same activity will help chill your buttons by decreasing your anxiety and increasing your belief that you got this, whatever "this" may be. When you lower your stress, you will feel calmer and be able to think clearly and creatively so you can make the best possible choice. It's basically the first step toward achieving Zen Master status. (Congrats! You have only 4,347 steps left to go!)

As with all of the practices I recommend in this book, it's easier said than done. It's not that it's hard to do just one thing at a time (unless, of course, that one thing is playing Candy Land). It's that most of our brains haven't practiced it enough. Here's a four-step process to get you started:

1. Notice that you're multitasking.

2. Remember that you can choose to do just one thing at a time instead.

3. Decide if now is the time to do just one thing.

4. Carry on, either way.

STEP 1: TRY TO REALIZE, WHENEVER POSSIBLE, THAT YOU'RE DOING MORE THAN ONE THING AT A TIME. If I'm not mistaken (and I'm not), this happens way more often than you think it does: Texting in the carpool line. Sneaking a quick scroll through Facebook while you're waiting for your kid to make her next move in Connect Four. Slathering sunscreen on small bodies while making lunches. Half listening to your spouse while you keep one eye on the season finale of *Queer Eye*. Before you know it, the parents in line behind you are honking, a nose-picking six-year-old has beaten you at Connect Four, you've smeared peanut butter on your kid's arm, and you've agreed to spend date night at the car show. DAMNIT! You bet your ass you're going to snap at the next tiny human who walks through the door. The point is, you can't choose not to multitask if you don't even realize you're doing it in the first place.

STEP 2: REMIND YOURSELF THAT YOU ALWAYS HAVE THE OPTION TO DO JUST ONE THING. This is always a possibility, no matter what you're doing. It's just about getting your mental awareness and physical actions on the same page, at the same time. If you are stressed, exhausted, or working on a particularly challenging or boring task, it may be especially hard to stay focused. Practice helps, and we'll talk more about how to practice single-tasking later in this chapter.

STEP 3: DECIDE IF NOW IS THE RIGHT TIME TO MULTITASK OR NOT. While it is always possible to do just one thing at a time, you don't have to be obsessive about it. There are definitely times when multitasking makes sense. I listen to audiobooks while I fold laundry, I knit in front of the TV, and I talk on the phone while I'm out for a walk. Here are a few questions that can help you figure out if it's a good time to multitask:

★ **Are you already tense, stressed, or tired?** If so, chances are good that you'll either drop a ball or lose your shit.

★ **Are there any significant ramifications if you screw up?** Yeah, maybe I space out for part of my audiobook or put my socks in my daughter's drawer. No big deal. But texting while you drive? Helping your kids with their homework while editing an important work document? Don't do that. You screw those up, you got potentially big problems.

★ **Are you with your kids?** Kids take up more space in our brain than we realize; it's like they open up all the tabs on the computer and the minute you try to open up even one more, the whole thing freezes up and smoke starts pouring out of the back of your laptop. This is a rough reality, whether you're a stay-at-home parent or your day is split between the office and the witching hours at home with the kids. Don't believe me? Pay attention the next time you try to tap out a quick text in the middle of a game of Uno or pay your bills while researching shin guards and soccer balls online. Notice your stress levels, and see if you lose it.

Yep. I thought so.

STEP 4: CARRY ON! And as you do, pay attention to how you're feeling and how things are going. Is multitasking still working for you? If so, you're good to go. If not, go back to Step 2.

Single-tasking when you're with your kids is extra tricky for parents who work from home, or have some flexibility in their schedule, but only if they're still available by phone, email, or text. There's no perfect solution to this double-edged sword, but here are a few options that may be helpful to any parent struggling with the challenges of trying to get stuff done while taking care of kids:

★ **Accept that you won't get everything done.** Give yourself a break. You're not failing at adulting or parenting if there are still dishes in the sink, appointments that haven't been scheduled, or friends you haven't called back. You're just being realistic about what you can and can't handle and making smart choices that help lower your stress and preserve your sanity.

★ **Set a timer for ten or twenty minutes**, and fully hang with your kid during that time. Then hook her up with a book, a game, or a show on Netflix—whatever it takes to keep her entertained so you can take care of business. (If your child is still taking naps, wait until she finally goes down.)

★ **Be intentional and transparent about your task switching** (which is what you're actually doing). "OK, once we've finished this puzzle, I need to take a break and answer these work emails. Once I'm done with that, I can come back and help you with the next one."

★ **Get thee some help.** Parents' helpers (children who aren't yet old enough to babysit but can entertain your kids while you work in the house) are a great option and usually much less expensive than an older babysitter. And if any sort of childcare isn't in your budget, trade for it. Community childcare co-ops can be organized online and make it easy to share the care.

★ **Teach your children to do chores.** This will take some time and energy on the front end, but it is well worth the investment, because it won't be long before they can start to take chores off your plate instead of just piling them on. Oh, and it's the way parenting has worked for about a bajillion years; no reason to end that trend now.

★ **Ignore the kids.** I'm not kidding. Teach and encourage them to entertain themselves. Let them be bored; it really is good for them. You don't have to be constantly attentive to your child, and you sure as hell don't need to involve yourself in their play. (For more on this, see Chapter 7.)

Making It Easier to Do One Thing at a Time

. . . .

Setting an intention to single-task is an important first step, but it may not be enough. If you've been practicing multitasking for a while now (which you have), your brain will get kind of itchy when you try to slow it down. Single-tasking will get easier with practice. In the meantime, here are a few ways to make it easier to stay focused when you need to:

★ **Remember that paying attention isn't about staying perfectly, unwaveringly attentive to whatever it is you're doing.** That's great when it happens, but don't stress when it doesn't. Just make a decision to do what you're going to do for as long as you need to do it, and when you notice your mind wandering (as it will, I promise!), come back to what you're doing.

★ **Get some sleep.** An exhausted brain is like a twitchy squirrel, eager to chase after everything, whether or not it's actually an acorn. The more you sleep, the easier it will be to do just one thing at a time, and do it well.

PRACTICE SINGLE-TASKING WHEN IT'S EASY

YOU'VE PROBABLY BEEN multitasking for years now, which means you're wired to do it. Changing a well-established habit isn't easy, so let's not make it any harder than it already is. Practicing any skill when we're *not* under pressure will make it far more likely that we'll be able to utilize that skill when the heat is on.

To that end, pick one or two activities you do every day that you enjoy (or at least don't despise), and just do those things. It may be drinking your coffee or tea, reading the morning paper, walking from the train to the office, or waiting in the school pickup line. Turn off the radio or TV, put away your phone, and each time you notice your thoughts wandering, bring your attention back to what you're doing.

For me, it's showering and reading to my kids. If I don't make a point to stay present, I get to the end of my shower, and my hair is wet but I have no idea if I've washed it. And as for the reading thing, well, I don't mean to brag or anything, but I can read an entire book out loud to my daughters while simultaneously dissecting a weird interaction with a friend or wondering if I remembered to nag my husband about the kitty litter or, you know, doubting my entire career path and life trajectory. So, that's fun. EXCEPT IT'S TOTALLY NOT, and by the time we get to the end of the book, I'm a ball of stress and self-doubt and my buttons are huge and bright and red, and I totally freak out at my kids when all they did was ask for another story.

★ **Write it down.** If some thought keeps distracting you, and you're worried you might forget it, write it down. Keep a pad of paper on the counter or your bedside table (and in the name of all things holy, do not freaking multitask in bed), and take a moment to jot down that little mind worm. I recommend using a good old-fashioned pen and paper because the task list app on your smartphone is a big old screen time sinkhole, and don't even pretend it's not.

★ **Narrate your experience.** Just say what you're doing, either silently or out loud. "I'm walking to the pantry to get the spaghetti. Now I'm filling the pot with water and putting it on the stove." I know this sounds nuts, but the more stressed or exhausted you are, the more helpful it will be. Narrating your experience will make it much more likely that you'll be thinking about what you're doing, which is way better than not thinking about what you're doing. Your stress will go down and your ability to remember to turn off the stove will go up.

Put Down Your Damn Phone

Smartphones and tablets are such a common cause of multitasking and parental meltdowns that they get their own special nod here. Your screen triggers you by showing you terrible news or reminding you of everything you haven't yet done for your boss or mother-in-law or that damn Jane from the PTA who needs to calm it down already. And even if you're reading or watching something hilarious or heartwarming, the minute your kiddo walks into the room it's going to feel like he's barging into your reality, which may be far more awesome than actual reality, which is extra annoying because you just want five more minutes to watch the end of that hilarious honey badger video and DAMNIT KID WHAT DO YOU WANT? and well, the next thing you know, you've lost your shit again.

> Getting some space from your phone is one of the most powerful changes you can make in your life and parenting.

Getting some space from your phone is one of the most powerful changes you can make in your life and parenting. So put it down. Actually, get it out of the room. (Research has found that just having the thing nearby—even if it's turned off—distracts us.) As long as they're anywhere near us, smartphones are the enemies of single-tasking and sanity, and the source of all kinds of stress.

If it feels hard to let go of your phone, it's not because you're weak or vulnerable, or at least not any more than the rest of us. The apps on our phones are intentionally designed to grab our attention and hold it firmly in place. Some of the smartest minds in the tech world are paid obscene amounts of money to figure out the most effective strategies to get us to spend as much time as possible in their apps. Just buying or downloading the app isn't enough for them; they want us to check it as often as possible. The more time we spend lining up three shiny gems or double-clicking pictures, the more likely we are to see the ads they post, and the more we see those ads, the more likely we are to click on them, and the more often we click on them, the more likely we are to buy whatever they're selling, and YAY for everyone except, well, us. But we don't have to fall for their evil ploys. We can take back our time and our minds without having to relinquish our beloved devices.

Here are a few tips to get you started; choose the ones that will be most helpful to you and start there.

★ **Chill out.** Remind yourself, and truly believe, that you don't need to read every single text, email, or headline the minute it lands in your phone. You really don't. You can deal with it later. There are very few, if any, situations in life that truly demand an immediate response. Yes, you might miss an update or last-minute playdate invitation every now and then, but the sanity you'll gain is well worth the trade-off.

★ **Turn off the beeps and buzzes.** As much as you may agree with my previous point, your brain is no match for your phone's notifications. So turn them off. Seriously. Your phone should not ding, buzz, light up, or vibrate for anything other than a phone call or text message.

★ **Make yourself unavailable.** Familiarize yourself with the Do Not Disturb (DND) mode and use it often. I have my phone set so only the most important calls (from my parents, husband, or the girls' school) come through when I'm working or with my kids. My phone automatically goes into DND mode each night from 9 p.m. to 7 a.m. so it won't bother me overnight.

★ **Put your phone to work for you.** Utilize your phone's settings that allow you to monitor and limit your own screen time. This feature (called Screen Time on iPhones and Wellbeing on Androids) provides statistics on exactly how much time you're spending on the various apps on your phone. In addition, you can set limits on how much time you can spend on each app before the app becomes harder to access for the rest of the day.

★ **Remove the distractions.** Delete any apps you don't truly need, especially the most addictive ones. I ditched Facebook, Twitter, and my favorite crossword puzzle app; I just can't be trusted with them. What are the apps that suck you in unnecessarily? Be honest and get rid of them.

★ **Pretend you're wired.** Pretend your smartphone is an old-fashioned phone, stuck to the wall. It used to be that when the phone rang, you had to stop what you were doing and walk over in order to answer it. Unless the cord was super long, it wasn't possible to wander around the house doing three other things while having a conversation. Take your phone out of your pocket and leave it where you might have put a wired phone. Walk over to it when you need to call or text; otherwise, leave it be.

★ **Don't use your phone for everything.** Even if you can. Go old school whenever possible. Put a radio on the counter so you don't have to reach for your phone each time you want some music. If you like to read ebooks, buy a dedicated device rather than reading from the app on your phone. Write your task list and take notes on a piece of paper or in a notebook.

★ **Wear a smartwatch.** This is a great option for folks who are concerned about missing an important call or notification but don't want to be distracted by everything else on their phones. Resist the temptation to download twenty-seven tiny games, turn off any unnecessary notifications, and leave your phone in the other room. Oh, and be sure to notice if your watch is yet another source of distraction. Be honest with yourself, and if this is the case, stop wearing it.

★ **Find something else to stare at.** It's not bad to have something to do while you wait for the doctor or take a little downtime whenever the kids are actually playing nicely. But smartphones aren't the same as magazines or newspapers; those shiny little screens grab our attention with a ferocity and tenacity that just doesn't happen with books, knitting, or in my husband's case, the ukulele. You'll find it easier to answer your kids' questions or move on to the next activity if you've been enjoying something less addictive than a constantly updating screen.

★ **Pick a default app that won't trigger you.** If you really can't stop yourself from reaching for your phone, then stick to apps that won't trigger you and are less likely to suck you in. There are no guarantees, of course, but we can make better and worse choices. News apps and social media are out. Meditation apps, ebooks, digital sudoku, crossword puzzles, and time-limited games are a better choice, unless you find yourself hiding in the bathroom trying to come up with a three-letter word for button pusher. If that's the case, delete them.

★ **Don't take your phone to bed.** The bright light from the screen makes it harder to fall and stay asleep, and exhaustion is a major trigger. More on this in the next chapter.

★ **In the name of all things holy, do not use your phone in the car.** Put it in the trunk if you have to. If you need GPS directions or a podcast for the kids, then set it before you pull out of the driveway and don't mess with it until you get to where you're going. And if the podcast ends before you get to your destination, then make the kids listen to the radio or even sit in silence. They'll survive, and in a few years they can write their college essays about it. Remember, it won't be long before they'll be driving themselves, and they're learning how to do it from you.

★ **Set aside specific times to stare at your phone.** You don't need to ditch it completely (although I do have some friends who went back to old-fashioned flip phones and were really happy about it). Find a few minutes when the kids are in bed or at school or you're between meetings and scroll away. Just remember that you're practicing something you might not actually want to get better at.

Whatever steps you decide to take, the end goal is to notice when you're distracted or trying to do too many things are once. Multitasking can be useful, but it's also a major trigger for most parents. Once you realize this, you can choose to ignore the laundry, set down your phone, and pay attention to whatever you're doing, even if it's just for a few minutes. Over the course of a day, these brief moments of focus will decrease your stress, increase your calm, and help you keep your shit together.

CHAPTER 5

Shit You Have to Do If You Don't Want to Lose Your Shit

SLEEP SLEEP SLEEP. YOU MUST SLEEP

★

THE VILLAGE IS NOT OPTIONAL

★

CUT YOURSELF A WHOLE LOTTA SLACK

Now that you're kicking ass at doing just one thing at a time, let's talk about exactly what you should be focusing your precious time and energy on. In this chapter, we're going to dive into the other three essential practices: sleep, support, and self-compassion.

Sleep
YOU NEED IT WAY MORE THAN YOU REALIZE

If you're getting enough sleep and feeling reasonably alert and energized, then that's awesome! Keep it up. But if you struggle with sleep or you're exhausted throughout the day, then keep reading.

Regardless of what you want to believe, you can't actually function on five hours of sleep each night. And no, you're not going to make up the sleep over the weekend. (Who are you kidding? You're a parent, remember?) And, in case you really need me to spell it out for you, sleep is most certainly NOT for when you're dead. (Your freshman year in college called; it wants its lame-ass joke back.)

HOW TO FUNCTION WHEN YOU'RE EXHAUSTED

IF YOU'RE NOT sleeping well on a regular basis, well, that stinks. I've been there, and I'm so sorry. Hopefully, whatever's keeping you up will ease up soon—you'll finish that big project for work, or the kid will learn to sleep through the night, or your spouse will stop snoring. Meanwhile, here are a few survival tips to get you through until that happens:

★ Accept that you are exhausted and that exhaustion is a real thing. Don't try to deny it or pretend that you can power through it.

★ Lower your expectations as much as possible. Take the nonessentials off your list until you get some rest. That might take a while. That's OK. It's a phase, and you can get back to the rest of your life once you're sleeping again.

★ Slow down as much as you can and focus on one thing at a time as often as you can. A tired brain is just not capable of multitasking.

★ Be transparent about your exhaustion. Tell your kids what's going on, and ask older kids for help. They'll be less likely to misinterpret your crankiness, and you'll be modeling skillful ways to manage fatigue.

★ Remember that as long as you're exhausted you won't be functioning at full capacity and you'll feel like a crazy person and you'll be more likely to lose your shit, so cut yourself a whole lotta slack, OK?

Sleep deprivation impacts every aspect of your emotional, psychological, and physical functioning. It messes with your judgment, clouds your thinking, screws up your mood, and makes you way more likely to lose your shit. You might as well be drunk, but not the happy, chill kind. You're the snappy, cranky, unaware, stupid, shit-losing kind of drunk.

There's a lot of advice out there about how to get more and better sleep, but at the end of the day (literally), just go all paleo on yourself. Pretend you're a cave person, sleeping in your dark little cave, only with more pillows and fewer saber-toothed tigers. Think about a caveman's schedule. Exercise, work, intellectual stimulation (you're a well-read cave person), and bright lights are for daytime. Nighttime is for chill and darkness and activities that do *not* light up your nervous system. Reading, crafting, playing cards, petting your cat, or working on a puzzle (if you can pull yourself away from it when it's time for sleep!) are all great choices. Needless to say, bright lights, intense shows, social media, and generally whipping yourself into an anxious frenzy ain't gonna cut it. *Capiche?*

Now before you get all itchy and defensive about your nightly Netflix, ask yourself this question: Is it working for you? This is not a theoretical question, I am legit asking. If you can honestly say that you are getting enough sleep at night and that you have enough energy during the day to do what you need to do, then keep on keepin' on. Drink your after-dinner espressos and spend an hour or two with your PlayStation. There's nothing wrong with that, as long as it's working. But if you are having a hard time with sleep and exhaustion, then you need to deal with it. Here are a few more ideas to get you started. (Bonus: These will be helpful for your kids too!)

MAKE SLEEP A PRIORITY. Put it right at the top of your list of Shit You Must Do If You Want to Keep Your Shit Together. This doesn't mean you'll instantly get a solid eight hours every night, but it does mean you're going to keep working on it.

BE HONEST WITH YOURSELF ABOUT HOW MUCH YOU ARE (OR AREN'T) SLEEPING. The easiest way to do this is to track it. Get yourself a nifty little wristband that tracks your sleep, or keep a notebook on your bedside table and jot down the time when you turn off the light and when you wake up. These measurements won't be super precise or accurate, but over time you'll start to see some patterns, including when you get more sleep or way less, and you might get some insights into what, exactly, is messing with your rest.

STICK TO A SCHEDULE AS MUCH AS YOU CAN. Go to sleep and wake up at the same time every day, including weekends. This is especially important if you've been struggling with sleep and you're trying to get back on track; our bodies and brains prefer predictability and routine, especially with sleep. Sticking to a schedule will be almost impossible if you work overnight shifts; again, do the best you can, and lower your expectations for yourself as much as you can when you're exhausted.

GET READY FOR BED BEFORE YOU'RE TOO TIRED TO GET READY FOR BED. Have you ever noticed how much harder it is to get your kiddo into his pajamas when he's exhausted? Well, same goes for you. There's a reason why it's so damn hard to get off your couch once you've gotten settled in for the evening, and it's not because you're lazy or the force of gravity is stronger in your living room. It's because you're exhausted, and an exhausted brain has a hard time motivating you to do even the most basic tasks, like brushing your teeth. So do yourself a favor and get everyone's pajamas on and teeth brushed as early in the evening as you can. It will make it easier to get to bed when the time comes.

GET THAT SCREEN OUT OF YOUR FACE. The blue light from your phone or tablet is super bad for your sleep cycles. Every time you lie in bed staring and scrolling, you might as well be shining a WAKE UP WAKE UP WAKE THE F*** UP alarm laser right into the depths of your brain. Any exposure to bright light in the evening messes with your circadian rhythms and makes it harder for you to fall asleep and sleep well, but that bright screen four inches from your face is the worst. Try reading a printed book instead, or if you really, really can't put down your screen, use an ebook reader instead of a tablet or a phone, and dim the screen as much as you can. There are a few different tricks and apps that can make the screen super dark but still visible; research your particular gadget for details.

USE YOUR BED FOR SLEEP AND SEX AND PRETTY MUCH NOTHING ELSE. A little light reading (of an actual printed BOOK) is cool, and beditation (meditation in bed, obvi) is never a bad thing, but don't you dare get cozy with your computer. You want your brain and body to associate your bed and bedroom with sleep, not spreadsheets and social media.

TAKE IT EASY WITH THE BEVERAGES, AND I'M NOT JUST TALKING ABOUT COFFEE. But as long as you mentioned it, you may not be as caffeine-tolerant as you'd like to think. Lots of folks (myself included) shouldn't have any caffeinated beverages after around 2 p.m. But that's not all, folks. Alcohol is a problem too. It's a central nervous system depressant, which means it works by shutting down your brain and nervous system. Although a drink or two may help you calm down enough to fall asleep, as the effects of the booze wear off and your brain comes back online, it screws up your sleep stages, and it might even wake you up in the middle of the night. The end result is that you wake up feeling exhausted, even if you think you slept straight through.

You want your brain and body to associate your bed and bedroom with sleep, not spreadsheets and social media.

So take it easy on the caffeine and alcohol, and, well, pretty much every other beverage while you're at it, unless you want to be up peeing all night long. Chances are your bladder ain't what it once was.

GET SOME SUPPORT. If you're caring for an infant or sick child, swap nighttime feedings with your parenting partner, if you have one. Send your kiddo to spend the night with a family member or babysitter, or trade sleepovers with another parent. These aren't long-term solutions, but they can be lifesavers in a crisis.

Most of these suggestions are fairly simple to implement, and they generally work well. However, if you're dealing with depression, anxiety, chronic insomnia, or a sleep disorder, you may need additional support. If you've made an honest effort to clean up your sleep habits and it's not working, get some help. Ask your doctor for a referral to a mental-health professional or sleep specialist; they have a lot more tricks up their sleeves.

Support
YOU. CANNOT. DO. THIS. ALONE.

I t is not possible for human beings to raise children on their own and not lose their shit. Hell, it's barely possible even with support, so don't make it any harder on yourself than it needs to be.

You need help. I need help. Even the parents who seem to perpetually have their shit together need help. It's not because we're lazy or incompetent. It's because we are wired to function together—the village is not optional. The sooner you stop telling yourself that you should be doing it alone or that there is some nobility in handling everything without asking for help, and the sooner you tap friends and/or family

> We are wired to function together— the village is not optional.

members for said help, the sooner you will realize how much easier parenting can be, and the sooner you will stop losing it quite so often.

Regularly and frequently spending time with friendly, supportive adults (could be your spouse, a good friend, or the nice parent at the playground) calms your nervous system, making your buttons smaller, dimmer, and decidedly less vulnerable to your child's antics. This happens in a few different ways.

★ Supportive parents (especially the ones who know you and your family) are a great source of relevant and realistic information and advice. As you feel more confident in your parenting abilities, you'll be less likely to stress out and freak out.

★ Your peeps will get you out of your head and back into reality. They'll tell you when you're being a dumbass or misunderstanding a situation or blaming yourself for something that isn't your fault. They'll reassure you that you're not the only one who loses their shit. This will go a long way toward helping you chill out.

★ Your nervous system automatically calms down when you're with another adult you trust and feel safe with. Parenting just feels easier when you know that you've got another set of competent hands on deck in case things fall apart.

★ Spending time with adults we like makes us happy. And when we're happy, we're not freaking out.

In addition to your parenting partner (if you have one), an ideal support system includes three groups of folks: your pro team, your crew, and your peeps. Sometimes these overlap, and sometimes they don't. Sometimes they're the same folks you hung out with before you had kids, and sometimes they're not. Either way, they're all important.

YOUR PRO TEAM
The Experts in Your Life

Let's start with your pro team, which includes anyone you either pay for their services or seek out specifically because of their professional expertise. I'm talking about doctors, therapists, lawyers, pediatricians, childcare providers, coaches, teachers, and your minister, priest, rabbi, or imam. Sometimes you have a choice as to who these people are, and sometimes you don't, usually because your damn insurance won't pay for out-of-network providers or because there's only one childcare provider between your house and your office. If that's the case, do the best you can with what you have. It's not ideal, but that's life.

However, if you *do* have a choice as to which professionals you invite onto your team, then try to find people who will support you in parenting the way you want to *and* call you out when you're headed in the wrong direction. You want someone you can build a relationship

YOU CAN'T TEACH YOUR CHILDREN EVERYTHING

"**YOU CAN'T TEACH** the girls everything. That's not your job." My grandmother, a high school math teacher who raised seven children, said that to me several years ago. I had been complaining about how hard it was to teach the girls to swim. Instead of telling me to work harder, she encouraged me to find someone else to do it. I signed them up for lessons, they eventually learned to swim, and I gained thirty minutes each week not being pushed to the brink of losing my shit. #Winning.

Even if you are a professional teacher, therapist, pediatrician, or camp director, it is *not* your job to teach, treat, or constantly entertain your kids. This sort of role confusion will increase the stress in your family and deprive your children of the opportunity to learn from others. Find the experts you trust and let them do their jobs.

Caveat: If you homeschool or provide ongoing home-based care for a child with a chronic illness or disability, it will be extra important for you to get support and take space for yourself whenever you can. (More on that in Chapter 7.)

with over time and whose expertise you trust when you don't know what to do. I'm not a medical doctor, but our pediatrician is, so when I don't know how to deal with my daughter's symptoms, I just do what she says. This may sound super obvious, but in the current culture of Perfect Parenting, it can be easy to feel like we should know everything. Try not to do that. Let go of that stress and let the actual experts help you.

YOUR CREW
They've Got Your Back

U p next: your crew. This is your extended community of local and like-minded parents you can call on in a pinch to pick up a prescription when you're home with a puking kid, or to hang out with your little one on the school playground when you're running late. Here are a few things you need to keep in mind about your crew:

DO NOT UNDERESTIMATE THE POWER OF THESE PEOPLE. They can save your butt six ways to Saturday, but you have to get over yourself and ask. Not only is there no shame in reaching out for help, but your request may be helpful to your friends as well. Each time my friends reach out to me, they're (a) reminding me that I'm not the only person who can't do this alone, (b) giving me an opportunity to pay it forward, and (c) giving me permission to ask them for help, which is surprisingly awesome.

YOU HAVE TO RECIPROCATE. Do not mistake your crew for a pit crew. It's not their job to swoop in and save your ass every time you're in a jam. That's not what it means to be part of a community. If you expect them to help out time and again without offering something in return, eventually they're going to stop answering your texts. Even if your car isn't big enough to help with carpools, you can walk all the kids to the park, host a playdate, or drop off some food on a sick day.

THESE FOLKS MIGHT BE YOUR PEEPS, BUT THEY MIGHT NOT, AND THAT'S OK. You can have different relationships with different people, and not everyone is going to be in your inner circle. You can still help each other out in a pinch.

YOUR PEEPS
(or, as my kids call them, your BFFs)

You have to find your peeps. These are the people who talk you off the ledge when you're about to let loose all over the science teacher, drag you off the couch when you just want to cry into your coffee, and answer your 10 p.m. texts without hesitating. They're the ones who don't clean up their house before you come over, a sweet little gift you didn't know you needed but are damn happy to receive.

A quick story about my Peepiest of Peeps. I was hanging at her house one day when my older daughter was about ten months old; her daughters were a couple of years older. I had been struggling with exhaustion, anxiety, and loneliness, and I just needed to connect with someone who got it. All I wanted to do was to drink coffee with my friend at her kitchen table, so I put my baby on the couch with her kiddos to watch a TV show. A few minutes later we heard a thunk and a cry; my daughter had rolled off the couch. She had landed on a soft rug; she was fine. I kissed her better, put her back on the couch, and went back to my coffee in the kitchen.

A couple of minutes later, it happened again. Thunk, cry. I went back in, kiss kiss, you're OK, back on the couch with you, back to the coffee and friend for me.

The third time it happened, my friend looked at me, and without a hint of judgment or sarcasm (honestly, I don't know how she did it, because I would have been laughing my ass off), gently suggested that perhaps my daughter wasn't ready to sit on the couch alone. She was right, of course. Damnit—I really wanted that coffee.

Those small moments are how you know you're with your peeps. They don't make you feel

These are the people who talk you off the ledge when you're about to let loose all over the science teacher, drag you off the couch when you just want to cry into your coffee, and answer your 10 p.m. texts without hesitating.

crazy or stupid, even when you are being crazy or stupid. They are real with you; your peeps will tell you when you need to take your kid to a speech therapist or to get evaluated for ADHD, for example, and they do it without making you feel like shit. If you feel calmer and more connected, confident, and empowered after hanging out with them, then they're your peeps. If, on the other hand, you find yourself feeling confused, ashamed, or doubtful after an afternoon at the playground with other parents, well, they might have been having a bad day, or perhaps these folks aren't your peeps after all. I'm not saying they're jerks or that you should never hang out with them again, I'm just saying they're not the first people you should call or text the next time you find yourself hanging up streamers for your Saturday night pity party.

BUT WHAT ABOUT YOUR FAM?

Let's take a minute to talk about where your family fits into all of this. In an ideal world, they're part of your peeps and your crew, but not your pro team. Seriously, even if your mom is a literacy specialist or your brother is an orthodontist, you are allowed to consult with them only in a pinch and to ask for a referral to someone else. Trust me on this one.

Sadly, most of our families aren't ideal. Some are amazing, some are colossally screwed up, and most are good enough. And sometimes, well, they're just not available to help. Either because of death, addiction, dysfunction, or any other number of reasons, they're not your peeps or your crew, and maybe you feel like you can't even trust your kids with them. This straight-up sucks. Not only do you not have their support, but you may be using some of your limited time and energy to manage their challenges. This is a significant trigger for many parents. (Pro tip here: Stay off social media on Mother's Day, Father's Day, and any other family-related made-up holiday. All those pictures of perfect parents and happy siblings will light up your buttons like nobody's business.)

It's OK—and may even be helpful—to be sad about it. Parenting without family support is a big loss. When you can accept that this is the hand you were dealt, spend a little time just sitting with it and maybe having a nice cry, and you won't feel so stuck. Then you can get back to connecting with your support system—your peeps, your crew, and your pro team.

HOW TO FIND (AND KEEP!) YOUR PRO TEAM, CREW, AND PEEPS

Let's talk about how to build and sustain your support system. You may be really good at this, you may have struggled with it your entire life, or like me, you may find that becoming a parent has opened up a whole new world of challenges, including figuring out who you want to connect with and just how to do it. Here are a few suggestions to get you started:

GET CLEAR ABOUT WHAT YOU WANT AND NEED. This is all about owning who you are, what works for you, and what triggers you. There are many different ways to offer and receive support, and you should make choices that make sense for you whenever possible. For example, I can't stand being late. It triggers me like crazy, and I'm far more likely to yell at the girls when we're rushing. I know this about myself, and I know there's not a lot I can do about it. When another mother asked if I wanted to carpool with her, I did the only reasonable thing an uptight mother would do. I stalked her. Not like "zoom lenses pointed at her bedroom window" stalked her, but I started noticing when she got to school in the mornings. Once I was reasonably confident that she tended to be on time, I agreed to the carpool. I'm not saying it's bad to be late; I'm just saying I

> There are many different ways to offer and receive support, and you should make choices that make sense for you whenever possible.

can't handle it. Better to say no to the carpool in the first place than agree to trade rides with someone who is frequently late. I'd just end up being snappy with my kids and super bitchy to the other parent. Not their fault, and definitely not cool.

This advice doesn't just apply to your crew. Owning your style and your shit will help you choose the right pro team (if and when you have a choice), and it will help you find your peeps. We're not in high school anymore, even if it feels like it sometimes. You may still feel left out or envious of other parents, but you're a grown-up now and you can choose not to get sucked into that BS. It's not about who's popular or rich or pretty or pushes the sweetest stroller. It's about the folks who can quote your favorite movie back to you without missing a beat, who make you laugh when you're feeling like crap, and who won't judge you when your kids are acting like total jerks at the playground. The sooner you own your style, the sooner you can find your peeps.

ASK FOR HELP. Folks aren't freaking mind readers, and they're just as busy trying not to lose it as you are. The worst that will happen is that they'll say no, which they are totally allowed to say. The best that can happen is that they'll say yes, which is great for all kinds of reasons.

SHOW UP. If you want to connect with your crew, you need to show up for them. Schedule your kids' medical appointments so you can take them instead of their nanny or grandmother. That's how you get to know your pro team. Pick your kids up from school if you can, and hang out on the sidelines at practice instead of sitting in the car and staring at your phone; that's where you'll find your crew. And if you're looking for more peeps, get your tushy to that Ultimate Frisbee game or religious service or book group. Go to your friend's fund-raiser. Drop off a meal for a neighbor who just had a baby. Text a silly GIF to a fellow parent who's having a rough day. The more you show up, the more connected you will feel to the people in your life, and the more connected they will feel to you.

> If you want to connect with your crew, you need to show up for them.

RESPECT YOUR BOUNDARIES. You can't help everyone all the time. It's not because you're a failure; it's because you're a human being with limited time and resources. Also, you won't click with everyone. There will always be people in your world who annoy, irritate, or straight-up trigger you. It may be fairly clear why; perhaps they remind you of an older sibling who used to bully you or you don't like how they talk to your kids. Or maybe you have no idea why they stress you out, and that's OK, too. Accept and honor it. It's OK to say no.

Repeat after me: It's OK to say no.

If that feels hard, just keep practicing. Say it until you believe it. Or pretend you're talking to your kids. I bet you've had a lot of practice saying no to them.

The alternative is to spread yourself way too thin, do too much for too many people and get yourself all stressed out and triggered and then come home and lose your shit all over your kids. So don't do that. Say no. Or no thank you. Or I'm sorry, I can't. Or I can't right now, but please ask again. Or just plain no. No. No. No.

If you can't do it for yourself, do it for your kids. Each time you say no to a request or an offer that doesn't work for you, you're lowering your stress, removing a trigger from your life, and making it less likely that you will lose your shit. You're also modeling appropriate limit setting for them.

BE KIND WHENEVER POSSIBLE. It's possible more often than you think. (I totally stole that from a random meme on Facebook, but it doesn't make it any less true.) What, you ask, does kindness have to do with not losing your shit at your kids? On the off chance you're not automatically pro-kindness (No judging here. Well, maybe a little judging here, but just a bit.), allow me to remind you that we get better at whatever we practice, whether it's playing the tuba or not being a jerk. Each time we're kind to someone, we're also practicing kindness, and before long it will become easier for us to be kind to ourselves and our children, which is the very reason you picked up this book in the first place, right?

Let me be clear about this: You can be kind *and* say no *and* hold your boundaries at the same time. Being kind isn't the same thing as being nice or always saying yes or throwing yourself under the bus. It just means not being a jerk about whatever is going on. (For the record, this is an excellent strategy to use with your kids; you can be kind to them and acknowledge their feelings and snuggle them even as you're holding the line on another cookie or a smartphone or a trip to the mall. Also, do kids even go to the mall these days?)

Oh, and while you're at it, be sure to add yourself to the list of people who deserve your kindness. You're worth it.

Self-Compassion

I f self-compassion sounds corny or weird to you, join the club. I'm the past president. In over a decade of studying psychology and social work, I never once heard those two words together. It wasn't until I started searching for strategies to curb my own shit-losing tendencies that I was introduced to the concept, at which point I rolled my eyes so hard they almost popped out of my head. All I could think of was Stuart Smalley, the *Saturday Night Live* character who sat in front of his mirror reciting his daily affirmations. (If you haven't seen it, google it. It's hilarious.)

Fortunately, that sort of syrupy-sweet forced self-love is not what self-compassion is about. Rather, it's about noticing that you're in the middle of a hard moment and making the choice to respond to yourself with a little warmth and kindness. It's about remembering that you're not the only one who loses their shit. Think about what your best friend would text you in response to a late-night SOS-I-can't-freaking-deal-with-this-parenting-crap message. That's the vibe you're going for.

> Each time we're kind to someone, we're also practicing kindness, and before long it will become easier for us to be kind to ourselves and our children.

This may sound super obvious when you read it here, but most of us never even realize (a) that we have internal monologues, (b) how downright abusive those diatribes can be, and (c) that there is another way to respond to ourselves. This was definitely the case with me; I spent years berating myself for being a terrible mother before I realized what I was doing. Fortunately, there is another way, a much better way. And no, you don't have to gaze at your own reflection all the

> It's easy to forget that the insanity that goes down in the rest of our lives impacts our parenting.

while reminding yourself that you're good enough, smart enough, and gosh darn it, people like you. (I told you to google it.) Instead, try these three steps, based on the work of Dr. Kristin Neff, a researcher and expert in self-compassion:

NOTICE THAT YOU'RE BEATING YOURSELF UP. The ability to notice is so powerful that we're going to dig into it in Chapter 8. You may be shocked to realize how often you mentally trash yourself. Don't ignore it, don't get sucked into it, and for goodness' sake, don't beat yourself up for beating yourself up. Just notice that you've had a rough moment and that you're being unnecessarily crappy to yourself in response.

RESPOND TO YOURSELF THE WAY YOU WOULD TO A GOOD FRIEND. Imagine what you might say if a close friend called you with all the details of a truly awful evening. They totally lost their shit, and they feel epically guilty and ashamed about it. I really hope you wouldn't respond with, "Yeah, you suck. You're a crap parent, and you're doing a shit job. Screw it—have you tried hunkering down with a pan of brownies and a bottle of wine and just not thinking about how everyone else is nailing this parenting gig and you're not?"

You wouldn't say that to someone else, so don't say it to yourself. Try a little kindness instead, perhaps something like, "It's OK. Raising small people is damn hard. I'm only human. Even good parents have bad moments. I'm going to take a few deep breaths, get a cup of tea, and remember that the kids will be alright." You may find that the brutal thoughts return. That's totally normal; just stick with the kindness. Fake it 'til you make it, and eventually, you'll start listening to yourself.

This is also a great time to remind yourself about any other stressors in your life. It's easy to forget that the insanity that goes down in the rest of our lives impacts our parenting. Our vision gets myopic when we're freaking out, so take a moment to get a little perspective on everything you've got on your plate. This isn't about making excuses or justifications; it's just an acknowledgment of the reality that you're dealing with. Not to get all philosophical on you, but hard situations make life harder. You're not parenting in a vacuum, and this is a great time to keep that in mind.

REMEMBER YOU ARE NOT ALONE. This one is a game changer. I have no clue how or why the human brain evolved to trick us into thinking that we're the only one who struggles and has awful moments, but it has. The next time your brain tries to convince you that you are the only one having a terrible day or week or month with your kiddo, DO NOT TAKE THE BAIT. Don't you dare chomp on that shiny little thought that will inevitably yank you out of the only place where you can actually breathe and leave you flipping and flopping on the dry land of loneliness. *You are not alone, and you sure as shit aren't the only parent who loses it with their kids.* Call your brother or your best friend or go see your therapist or go back and read Chapter 2 of this book or google "how to stop yelling at my kids" and remember that there wouldn't be 83 MILLION results (for reals) if you were the only person struggling with this. You are not a freak or a failure. You are a human being. Welcome to the club. We're happy to have you.

If you've never practiced self-compassion, it's going to feel super weird the first time you try it. It's kind of like trying to speak in a language that you barely know. You're going to have a hard time finding the right words, and even then, you'll still stumble over your own tongue when you try to say them. Hang in there. It'll get easier with practice. Here a few things to keep in mind along the way:

★ **If the words just won't come, try *doing* something nice for yourself.** If your kids are around and awake, do the best you can. Say something to them like, "Hey, kiddos, I'm feeling a little cranky, so I need a little quiet time. Why don't we all take a break for a few minutes?" Then put them in front of a book or screen and snuggle in with a blanket or your favorite book or journal. Make yourself a mug of something warm and yummy. Text a friend who always has your back and cracks you up. Lie down on the living room floor and stretch out your body. Turn on your favorite song or look at a picture of a sweet moment when none of you were losing your shit.

★ **Remember that kindness is a skill**, just like throwing a Frisbee or grilling or not losing it. And just like every other skill, the more you practice it, the better you'll get at it. If it feels too challenging to have compassion for yourself, start with the folks around you. Practice

ADVANCED KINDNESS PRACTICE

IF YOU WANT to kick your kindness practice up a notch, try a form of meditation called *metta*. *Metta* means "loving-kindness," and the practice comes from the Buddhist tradition. However, it is completely secular, or it can be adapted to your own spiritual or religious practices. *Metta* is the silent repetition of kind wishes to yourself and others. There are several variations, but here's what I say:

May I be happy. May I be healthy. Maybe I be safe. May I live with ease.

When I'm super frustrated with my kiddos, I'll send a little *metta* their way: May you be happy. May you be healthy. May you be safe. May you live with ease. May you give me a little space so I don't strangle you.

(Even if I don't feel loving toward them at that moment, practicing *metta* helps me calm down, focus my thinking, and at the very least, distracts me from the angry rants that bring me even closer to losing my shit.)

You can also send *metta* to your grandmother, the letter carrier, or your pet hamster. It's not about the recipient; it's about the act of offering compassion. You can do this when you're alone or while you're hanging out with your kiddos or just hanging on by a thread.

You can think about *metta* like batting practice for kindness. If you want to get really good at hitting a baseball, you go to the batting cages and hit ball after ball. You want to get really good at kindness? Practice it over and over again; it all starts with our thoughts, which influence our behaviors. Oh, and there's an added bonus: *Metta* is a great way to simplify and focus your thoughts and calm down a jangled nervous system.

kindness when it's easy—it can be as simple as just looking up, smiling, and saying hi to the checker at the grocery store. The more you smile at strangers, the easier it will be for you to be kind (including to yourself) when all you want to do is throttle someone. It sounds crazy, but it works.

★ **If you're having a hard time speaking the language of compassion, spend time with people who can help you get more fluent.** Connect with folks who will respond to your challenges with support and understanding. It might be a cousin or your minister or a parent at your child's preschool. It doesn't really matter who it is, as long as that person responds to you with compassion and acceptance and doesn't go all Judgy McJudgerson when you tell them about your latest parenting shenanigans.

★ **Practice when it's easy.** We've already talked about this in Chapter 4, and it's worth repeating. You are going to need all the self-compassion you can get when you lose your shit (more on that in Chapter 9), which is precisely when it's going to be hardest to muster. Treating yourself with kindness in the face of smaller gaffes and missteps will help prepare you for the most challenging moments.

Come back to compassion whenever you can. It will help you calm down after the meltdown, and it will also make it way less likely that you'll lose it with your kids in the future. Kindness pulls from your prefrontal cortex (your adulting brain), and as you bring that part of your brain online, you're turning down the power to your limbic system, the crazy toddler bouncing around inside your skull. This will help shrink your buttons, which means you'll be less sensitive the next time your child sticks out their finger, ready to push.

CHAPTER 6

Shit You Should Do If You Don't Want to Lose Your Shit

STOP THINKING

★

START MOVING

★

SLOW YOUR ROLL

The fun's not over, folks, because I've got seven more practices that will help you stay calm when your little button pusher comes at you. I want you to think of these as Optional, But Not Really. Every one of them will help you get your shit together, so for maximum awesomeness, you should do as many of them as you can as often as you can. In no particular order, these are Simplify, Stretch, Seek Silence, Slow Down, Space from Your Kids, Say Thank You, and Breathe. (You can also go with Suck Air if you really want to stick with the "S" theme.)

I'm sure you've been thinking that you should probably do more of these things more often anyway, and now I've got an extra incentive to get you going: You'll be less likely to lose your shit with your kids.

Simplify
CALM YOUR SHIT DOWN

Clutter of any sort is a trigger, plain and simple. Too much stuff, too many choices, too many plans, too much information, and too many thoughts overwhelm our systems and put us on edge. We get stressed when there are too many balls in the air (or on the floor), even if those balls don't require our attention at the moment or aren't directly relevant to our lives yet have wormed their way into our awareness anyway.

Simplifying your life will help you feel calmer and less triggered. While many folks associate a simpler life with less stuff, it doesn't stop there. As a stressed-out parent, you can also benefit from:

★ Reducing the number of choices and decisions you have to deal with on a regular basis

★ Clearing your schedule and reducing your obligations

★ Reducing the amount of information you take in

★ Calming and focusing your thoughts

PHYSICAL CLUTTER
Is All That Stuff Making You Lose Your Shit?

Decreasing the physical clutter in your house is a great place to start. The less crap you have around, the less crap you have to deal with, the easier it is to find what you need when you need it, and the more money you will have for stuff or experiences you really want or need to spend it on. And even when you're not dealing with the crap, just seeing it can stress you out. There are a million books and websites focused on decluttering; pick one that you like and do what it says.

> Simplifying your life will help you feel calmer and less triggered.

HOW TO CUT DOWN ON THE KID CRAP

SOME PARENTS FIND it easy to control the kid clutter. I am not one of them. If you aren't either, here are some suggestions for dealing with the debris of life with little ones.

★ Resist the urge to show your love with stuff. Equating affection with gifts probably isn't the life lesson you want to teach your children, and too many toys can make it hard for kids to figure out what to play with and how to play with it.

★ When the kids are younger, declutter when they're not around. Don't give away their loveys or other truly special toys, but other than that, have at it.

★ As the kids get older, teach them how to declutter. Any junk they refuse to let go of has to stay in their room, or their half or third of the room.

★ Have a family declutter day. When everyone pitches in, your kids won't feel like you're picking on them.

★ If your child is having a hard time giving up something that they no longer use or wear, try for a compromise. Have them put it in a box labeled with their name and the date. Stick it in the closet, attic, or basement, and if they haven't asked for it in a year, talk to your kiddo about it, and then toss it. If it's still too hard, try for another year.

★ Put a donation box in the back hall or pantry, and challenge the family to put one item in it each day or week. Once the box is full, take the kids (and the box) to your local donation center.

★ Stop with the birthday party goody bags! If we parents band together, we can start a cultural revolution and rid the earth of this evil scourge. (And yes, this is a pet peeve of mine, in case that wasn't immediately obvious.)

CHOICES
They're Not As Helpful As You Think

Too many choices and decisions are another major source of clutter and stress in our lives. We think we want more options, but we don't. There are two ways in which having to make too many decisions wears us out and leaves us triggered. The first is called the Paradox of Choice. We assume that if we have more options, we'll pick the best possible one. WRONG. The more choices we have, the more we doubt what we've chosen and wonder if we should have picked something else. Ultimately we're just not as happy with what we ended up with. (This is why so many people like Costco. Need a vacuum? Fine—here's a decent one at a reasonable price. Buy it and be happy, and be sure to grab a soft pretzel on the way out.) The trick here is to learn to *satisfice*, which is just a fancy word for deciding that something is good enough. In most cases,

> The more choices we have, the more we doubt what we've chosen and wonder if we should have picked something else.

good enough is better than perfect, because perfect doesn't actually exist and you'll make yourself nuts trying to find it.

The next problem is called Decision Fatigue. Having to make too many decisions in a day, even seemingly simple or unimportant ones, wears us out and makes it harder to make future decisions. Our prefrontal cortexes (PFCs) haven't yet evolved to work that hard for that long, and they get tired. This is why we find ourselves staring blankly into the refrigerator, completely incapable of deciding what to make for dinner. Mac 'n' cheese again, any-one? In addition to getting rid of the stuff in your house, think about limiting the number of options you have to choose among and choices you have to make in a day. Here's how:

> Try to notice when you're repeatedly struggling with a decision or choice, and see if you can find a calmer, less stressful time to figure it out.

★ **Notice where you tend to get into choice battles with your kids, and limit the options.** Pick just one style of sippy cup, one pair of sneakers, or one flavor of jelly and stick with it as long as it's working. Remove the off-season cloth-ing from your kids' drawers, and ditch the books or toys that make you crazy. (This will work only when the kids are young, so enjoy it while you can.) Variety is the spice of life only as long as it's not causing you to lose your shit.

★ **Let go of as many decisions as you can.** Let your kids or parent-ing partner make the choices in their lives that you don't care about or mostly don't care about. And if you can't identify any, then you need to stop caring so freaking much already! Everyone craves self-autonomy, especially children, who spend much of their day being bossed around by grown-ups. When they're young, let them choose when you don't care about the outcome. (Green or blue under-wear? Piano practice or bathtime first? Panera or California Pizza Kitchen?) As they get older, let them make more and more decisions and deal with the consequences. Either way, stop holding all the responsibility for everything in your family's life.

★ **Make choices when it's easier to do so.** It's hard to make decisions when you're tired or rushing out the door or being relentlessly nagged by a cranky kid, so put a plan in place before that happens. Schedule your meals for the week on Sunday night or Tuesday morning or whenever you have ten minutes to breathe and think. Have your kiddo pick out their clothes the night before. Try to notice when you're repeatedly struggling with a decision or choice, and see if you can find a calmer, less stressful time to figure it out.

★ **Remove the choices altogether.** Make the rules and tattoo them on your forehead or hang them on the wall if you have to. We have a No Screen Time on Saturdays policy in our house. This is nonnegotiable, and it means that my husband and I don't have to spend our precious weekend time and energy debating whether the girls can watch *Barbie's Life in the Dreamhouse* (which, for the record, is funnier than you expect). By the way, rules aren't just for kids, as I learned from a fellow mother. I had invited her to come to an evening event at school, and she politely declined by explaining that she just doesn't go out at night during the week. Rather than being offended, I was impressed and inspired by her ability to honor her own needs and communicate them clearly and respectfully.

DOING TOO MUCH
Your Schedule Is Making You Crazy

The third source of clutter that will absolutely trigger you is trying to do too much. Too many errands, obligations, extracurricular activities, and other plans. Not only is chronic busyness not good for your overall functioning and happiness, but it's not so great for your kids either. They need rest and downtime as much as you do, and they're likely to react to the stress the same way you do—with a massive meltdown. Here are a few suggestions for simplifying your schedule:

★ **Don't say yes just because you can.** It's OK to politely decline yet another invitation to a birthday party or parent social for no good reason (just don't say that second part). You can offer to schedule a play-date for another time if you want to, but you don't have to.

★ **Consider the big picture.** Each time you go to put something on your schedule, look at the rest of your week or month. How's it all looking? If you're booking a big event, or you're super busy, try to be extra thoughtful about what you're adding to your schedule.

★ **Go easy on the kids' extracurriculars.** A good rule of thumb is two activities per week. You choose one, and your kiddo chooses one.

★ **You don't need to be at every practice or rehearsal.** Set up a carpool. Drop the kid off and go run an errand or grab yourself a cup of coffee. (I know, I know, that's where you're supposed to connect with your crew. It's all about balance, people.)

★ **Remember that your schedule will change as your kids get older.** You can't do everything now, but in a few years, you'll be able to do more.

★ **Let it go.** You're not going to get everything done now. If you keep putting something on your list week after week, maybe it's time to move that item to a different list, perhaps Shit That Will Get Done Once the Kids Move Out.

TOO MUCH INFORMATION
You Really Don't Need to Know Everything

We live in an era of overwhelming information. This isn't always as awesome as it seems. Unnecessary, contradictory, or upsetting information will confuse and distract you, thereby increasing your stress. Remember that news notification on my cell phone about the national emergency that I told you about in Chapter 1? Yeah. I really didn't need that update, thankyouverymuch. You just don't need as much information as you think you do. I promise. Try some of these changes and see what you think:

★ **Pick one or two news sources** and check in with them a couple of times a day, not more. I listen to radio news while I drive to and from school each day. I have a friend who reads a real actual newspaper every morning, and that's it. If you feel compelled to watch TV news (please don't),

> The next time you find yourself scrolling and tapping, pay attention to how you're feeling and what you're thinking.

calm down with the twenty-four-hour business. Unless you're brokering peace in the Middle East or tracking a tornado across the plains, you really don't need constant updates.

★ **Social media** works for some folks but not everyone. The next time you find yourself scrolling and tapping, pay attention to how you're feeling and what you're thinking. Do you feel happier and more connected? Or are you feeling anxious, confused, annoyed, or otherwise triggered? Such responses are reasonable given the nature of social media; you never know when you're going to scroll your way into a Perfect Parent Picture or news of an untimely death or an awful headline that might not even be accurate or current but triggers you nonetheless. I'm not saying you should never check your social media accounts again (although I do have friends who have ditched social media altogether and are quite happy with the results); I'm just saying that if it's a trigger for you, try to be thoughtful about when and where you log on, and maybe do it less often.

★ **Be selective about what you expose yourself to.** My daughters recently asked me what the F-word is. I said I would tell them, but that once the word was in their brain, they wouldn't ever forget it and they might accidentally say it—and if they said it at school, they'd end up in the principal's office even if they didn't mean it. After a fair amount of bickering, the girls decided they didn't want to know. I share this story because the same is true for adults as well. Don't read and watch stuff you don't want in your brain. Don't want to think about all the horrible shit people do to each other? Stop watching *Law & Order: SVU*. Need a break from national politics? Put down the news magazine with the in-depth exposés on politicians. While this is no guarantee that you won't have anxious or upsetting thoughts, it's a powerful place to start.

> While you can't control what you're thinking, you can choose how you respond to whatever shows up in your mental landscape.

TOO MANY THOUGHTS
Your Brain Needs to Chill

Finally, simplify your thoughts. Even if you were to completely sanitize your environment and never watch anything more stressful than *PAW Patrol*, your thoughts will still get the best of you. You may be doing something as benign as wiping down the counter when all of a sudden you're overwhelmed by regretful, worried, doubtful, or confusing thoughts. You may be able to identify what triggered this sort of thinking, or maybe it came out of nowhere. Either way, this sort of mental upheaval is likely to increase your stress, amp up your buttons, and put you at risk of losing your shit with your kids.

> The trick is noticing when your mind is misbehaving in the first place.

As annoying as it may be, this sort of unpredictable thinking is completely normal and very common. While you can't control what you're thinking, you can choose how you respond to whatever shows up in your mental landscape. Many folks don't even realize that this is an option; they spend their days at the mercy of their restless minds.

The trick is noticing when your mind is misbehaving in the first place. Are you mucking around in an unpleasant memory, imagining something that may never happen, or judging yourself or your child in ways that aren't helpful? From there, can you get a little perspective on your thoughts and simply notice that they're happening? Can you remind yourself that thoughts aren't reality, and you don't have to treat them as such?

It's the difference between being an actor in a terrible play or an observer in the audience. Once you step off the stage, you can choose if you want to stay for the rest of the show or not. The possibility that we don't have to believe everything we think can be confusing, but it will become clearer and easier to do the more your practice.

Proponents of mindfulness (which is basically what I'm talking about here) argue that the ability to get a little perspective on, and space from, our own mental chatter is crucial for a calmer, happier existence, and I agree with them. The ability to redirect my awareness and thoughts has been a game changer for me; whenever I notice myself stewing in frustration or confusion, I sing a song, count my breaths, or remind myself that parenting is hard, and that I can do hard things. By the way, you can too.

There are many excellent books on mindfulness and meditation that you can check out. Meanwhile, here are some of my most effective strategies for stepping off a carousel of unhelpful thoughts:

★ Focus on what you're doing. (Narrating your experience can help.)

★ Sing your favorite song.

★ Count to eight or eighty-eight or anything in between, and then start again from one.

★ Recite your favorite poem or joke.

★ Repeat a prayer or mantra.

★ Learn how to meditate. This is the explicit practice of noticing your thoughts and choosing not to get caught up in them. (More on this in Chapter 8.)

★ Find something to be grateful for. (More on this shortly.)

No matter what you choose to think, your mind is still going to wander and come up with some bonkers memories or fantasies or fears that come out of nowhere. That's not because you're crazy; it's because our brains are wired to think all the thoughts all the time. You don't need to stress about this or try to control it. The trick is to remember that at any point, you can take a step back, notice what you're thinking about, and decide whether or not you want to keep hanging out with those thoughts. It's a small shift in your awareness but a deeply powerful one.

Stretch
YOU. MUST. MOVE. YOUR. BODY.

B y stretch, I don't just mean touch your toes, although that counts too. I mean move your body. Go for a walk. Do some push-ups. You can even get all religious about your Barre class or marathon training (just don't expect to see me there). The point is that You. Must. Move. There are many ways to understand how physical movement works to calm down your jacked-up nervous system but at the risk of oversimplifying, we'll stick with two.

When you are triggered for any reason, your body releases stress hormones as part of the Fight, Flight, Freeze, or Freak Out reaction. Exercise reduces the levels of those hormones in your body and increases the neurochemicals that decrease pain and heal your body. Less stress + less pain = less shit loss.

> Choosing not to explode can be a very skillful choice, but it's not always enough to bring our body down off High-Alert Status.

In addition, each time you're triggered, your nervous system gets all jacked up, ready to kick ass, run away, freeze everything out, or lose some shit. When your nervous system can't do one of those things, it gets even twitchier. This is because it can't necessarily tell the difference between *not being able* to react and *choosing not* to react. Not being able to take action, for any reason, in the face of real or perceived danger can be traumatizing. Choosing not to explode can be a very skillful choice, but it's not always enough to bring our body down off High-Alert Status. If your body is super tense or wants to move, then move it. It can't tell the difference between running away from a grizzly bear and running around the neighborhood; it's just happy to finally do that thing it's been trying to get you to do all along.

To top it all off: More exercise will make you less anxious and depressed, more fit, and generally healthier. Again, there are approximately one bajillion books, videos, podcasts, websites, and apps devoted to getting you to get off your tushy. Pick the one that works for you, and do what it says. Also, keep these ideas in mind:

DO WHAT YOU LIKE. Some people prefer mindful movement, such as yoga or tai chi, while others run, lift weights, or do circuit training. Some folks like to work out alone, others prefer classes at the gym.

I have a friend who spends time each week swinging on a trapeze; I would rather poke my eye out with my daughter's favorite pencil, but it works for him and that's what matters.

THINK BIG AND SMALL. Getting your heart rate up and sweating through your shirt will not only calm your buttons down big-time, but you can also feel all awesome and self-righteous about it, which is cool. But don't underestimate the importance of smaller movements that you can do throughout the day, such as lifting and lowering your shoulders, stretching out your calves on the porch step, and walking up and down the driveway or stairs. Any physical movement can be helpful in both preventing parental explosions and calming yourself both mid-meltdown and after the storm has passed.

ASK A FRIEND TO WALK OR GO TO THE BATTING CAGES WITH YOU. Not only will you be more likely to get the exercise you need because you don't want to be that jerk who always bails, but you'll be connecting with your support system too. Bonus!

MAKE IT FUN WITH TECHNOLOGY. I wear a fitness tracker on my wrist, and I get far more excited than a reasonable adult should when the screen lights up with a little fireworks display each time I reach my goal. Also, I'm connected to a bunch of random people through the app, and I hate it when they've gotten more steps than me. That ridiculous competitive streak is enough to get my ass out of bed in the morning to go for a walk. My husband has an app that keeps track of his workouts, and he hates to break a streak.

Seek Silence
ALL THAT NOISE IS MAKING YOU CRAZY

· ·

Noise is absolutely a trigger for many folks. Thanks to smartphones and wireless headsets and portable speakers, many of us are surrounded by sound every waking (and sometimes even sleeping) minute of every day. And that's just the noise we choose to turn on; it doesn't include the racket of traffic, alarms, barking dogs, obnoxious coworkers, and kids who cannot for the life of them remember to use their freaking indoor voices.

Spending time in silence even for a few minutes every day is crucial for our sanity for a number of reasons, including lowering our stress levels and cooling down our buttons. It can feel uncomfortable at first because your brain might try to compensate for the lack of noise by turning up the volume on your thoughts, but even that will get easier as you practice choosing how to respond to the ramblings of your mind.

Here are some ways to turn down the noise in your environment:

TURN OFF THE TV AND RADIO. If you're in the habit of having them on in the background, try muting the sound or turning them off for a few minutes at a time. And for goodness' sake, turn off the damn news.

SILENCE YOUR PHONE. The activity tracker I wear on my wrist vibrates for incoming texts or messages, so I never have to listen to my phone buzz, beep, or ring. If you don't want to wear a smartwatch or something similar, set your phone to Do Not Disturb when you want a little quiet time. You can add VIPs (your spouse, your job, or your kids' school, for example) to your Favorites list and set it so those calls will come through.

And, again, turn off those damn notifications. Do it now.

STOP TALKING. I'M NOT KIDDING. ZIP IT. Ask your kids to do the same. Quiet Time is a thing in our family, especially in the car when we have Quiet Rides. And yes, it is absolutely code for "Somebody is about to lose her shit, and it's probably Mommy." My girls have even started requesting Quiet Rides from time to time, and I'm always happy to comply.

Slow Down
YOU'RE NOT AS LATE AS YOU THINK

nless you're about to miss a flight or you're Spider-Man saving the world, you really don't need to hurry so often. Rushing sends a message to our brains and nervous systems that we need to kick into flight mode, whether or not we actually do. Sometimes we hurry when we're triggered, but sometimes we trigger ourselves by racing through the moment. So just don't. Try doing this instead:

TRY TO NOTICE WHEN YOU'RE RUSHING. If you are, take a moment to get real with yourself about whether or not you're really in a hurry or if you're just in the habit of moving faster than you need to.

TRANSITIONS ARE HOT SPOTS FOR UNNECESSARY RUSHING. We parents get all wiggy about how poorly our kids manage transitions without stopping to consider that we can be pretty bad at them too. Notice what happens each time you're leaving the house or switching activities, and slow that train down whenever you can.

GIVE YOURSELF MORE TIME THAN YOU THINK YOU NEED, especially if you're with your children. Remember that it takes kids FOR-FREAKING-EVER to zip up their jackets and tie their shoes, so give them at least ten minutes to finish what should take approximately forty-five seconds. At the very worst, you'll arrive a few minutes early and have time to go to the bathroom or grab a snack before your appointment.

DEAL WITH YOUR CHRONIC LATENESS. If you're always late, either get it together and don't do that anymore or just accept that you're chronically late and write it off as a midlife quirk or genetic defect or whatever. Either way, stop rushing. If you're going to be late whether or not you rush, then don't rush and be late anyway. Just don't ask me to carpool.

Say Thank You
GRATITUDE IS WAY MORE AWESOME THAN YOU REALIZE

Y ou've heard of gratitude by now, and either you're super skeptical or you know how amazing it is. I spent years dismissing and/or openly mocking this popular practice, but now I'm a believer. My conversion happened in the same place where almost everything in my life happens these days: my kitchen.

I really don't like making the girls' lunches each morning. I spent years grumbling about this boring, irritating, repetitive chore that I have to do just about every damn day.

And then one morning, for no clear reason, I suddenly realized how lucky I am. I'm so lucky to have enough money to buy the food we need and to live near a well-stocked grocery store filled with fresh fruits and prepackaged pretzels. After a childhood spent eating room-temperature sandwiches from brown paper bags, I marveled at the existence of reusable ice packs and insulated lunch boxes. I thought about how I'm healthy enough to get up each morning and walk down the stairs without any help, and how my girls are healthy enough to eat and digest a wide range of foods (not that they always agree to do so, but that's a different issue).

I still don't *enjoy* making lunches, but getting a little perspective and realizing how much worse it could be makes it so much easier. What I've realized since that morning is that gratitude can make almost every difficult parenting experience easier. Finding something to appreciate calms my anxiety and frustration, focuses my thinking, helps me get perspective, and makes it way less likely that I'll explode at my kids. Here are three simple steps for saying thank you in a tough moment:

1. Recognize that you're in a negative headspace. It's easy to get so caught up in your cranky, anxious, or irritated thoughts that you may not even realize you're having them. Noticing those thoughts is the first step toward changing them.

2. Find something to appreciate. If you can find something that has to do with whatever you're struggling with, that's great, but it's not necessary. You can be grateful for *anything*, including the fact that your house hasn't been struck by lightning recently, your teeth didn't just fall out of your face, and we live in an age of toilet paper and microwaves.

3. Repeat Steps 1 and 2 as often as necessary.

Breathe
IT'S YOUR SECRET SUPERPOWER

hate it when people tell me to breathe. It triggers my inner bitchy adolescent self, and it's all I can do to not bite their heads off. This is a rather unfortunate reaction on my part because it's actually

STRAP ON YOUR OWN MASK FIRST

IF YOU'VE EVER been on a plane, you've heard the instructions to strap on your oxygen mask first before helping children with theirs. If you pass out, you can't do anything for them. The oxygen mask rule is a popular metaphor for self-care in parenting, and it's easy to see why. Self-care is nonnegotiable if we want to have a snowball's chance in hell of being present and patient with our kiddos. While I don't love the idea of waiting until it feels like the plane is going down before you start caring for yourself, it's a great strategy when you're about to lose your shit. When you are freaking out and it feels like the plane is going down, reach for that oxygen mask and BREATHE.

great advice. Our breath is the only aspect of our sympathetic nervous system (the one that activates the Fight, Flight, Freeze, Freak Out response) that we can consciously control. Each time you breathe intentionally, you're hacking your nervous system and telling your buttons that everything is OK and they can chill already.

Breathing is also awesome because it's free, you know how to do it, and you can't get it wrong. Don't get all hung up on how long you should inhale for and which nostril you should exhale out of. Fast, shallow breaths aren't helpful, but as long as you're doing some version of slower and deeper, you're doing it right. You can breathe anywhere, anytime, without anyone knowing that you're trying not to lose your shit. You don't have to bust out your prayer beads or drop into downward dog on the floor of the pediatrician's office. All you have to do is inhale and exhale and only you will know that you're breathing your way off a ledge.

Finally, it's totally legit to consciously breathe your way through the day, especially if you're exhausted or stressed or unable to take space from your little button pusher. Hang in there, and keep on breathing. If nothing else, it's a powerful reality check. As long as you're breathing, you're OK.

There you have it, folks. We've made it through ten of the eleven BuRPs (aka Button Reduction Practices, or the Shit You Gotta Do if You Don't Want to Lose Your Shit). These practices will make your buttons smaller, dimmer, and much less available to your children, and they'll help you recover after you've lost it too. Do what you can to integrate them into your life, and when you forget (as you will), take a few deep breaths and come back to self-compassion. That's your first step toward getting back on the BuRP wagon.

> Noticing is crucial; if you're not aware of what's happening, you can't make the choice to do something differently.

The key move for each of these practices is *noticing*. Notice that you're exhausted, or doing thirteen things at once, or scrambling when you have plenty of time, or that you've been holding your breath for the better part of a decade. Noticing is crucial; if you're not aware of what's happening, you can't make the choice to do something differently.

We're going to talk a lot more about all of this noticing business in Chapter 8. One of the first things I want you to notice is how much time you're spending with your kids, and whether or not you need a little (or a lot) more space.

CHAPTER 7

Get Some Space from Your Kids So You Don't Lose Your Shit with Them

HOW TO
GET AWAY
FROM YOUR
KIDS

★

EVEN WHEN
YOU'RE
WITH THEM

There's one more strategy we need to discuss before we dive into what to do when you're about to lose your shit. I'm talking about spending less time with your kids. Or, more specifically, getting more intentional about the time you do spend with them.

This may sound counterintuitive, but taking a little time away from your kids is a highly effective way to not lose your shit with them for two different reasons:

1. You can't explode at your kids if you're not actually with them. Boom. Done.

2. Getting a little space will help cool your buttons so they're less vulnerable to being pushed, and it will help you calm down more quickly after you've lost it. The more triggered you are, or the more frequently or intensely you've been melting down, the more time and space you may need.

As compelling as these arguments may be, I'm guessing some of you still aren't convinced. Stick with me.

Today's parents spend more time with their children than any previous generation. This is true even for those parents with full-time jobs. At first glance, all of this quality time may seem like a good thing, but I'm not so sure. A strong, flexible connection isn't about constant togetherness. Think about the people you love most in the world other than your kids—your spouse, siblings, parents, or best friends. Do you want to spend every waking minute with them? Do you want them up in your face all the time, asking if you need help with something or if they can join your game? Unless you're still in the honeymoon phase, the answer is probably NOPE. You want

> A strong, flexible connection isn't about constant togetherness.

to see them regularly, maybe take a vacation, go for a walk, or enjoy a meal together, but you also want time apart, to hang out with other friends or just be alone with your thoughts, a good book, or favorite hobby.

The same is true for our relationship with our kids. Some of us go through a honeymoon phase when they're infants, which fortunately happens to be when they need frequent adult physical contact. As our kids grow, however, they need both physical and psychological space from us. They need time to get to know themselves, to gain the confidence that can come only from learning how to solve problems on their own, whether it's how to make a fort out of a cardboard box or resolve a fight with a friend or sibling. And our kids need to spend time with other adults, to learn how to be flexible as they adapt to different communication styles, rules, and expectations.

Our children don't need us constantly by their sides. That sort of continuous attention can feel intrusive and irritating. Rather, they need us to attune to their needs, to notice when they're calm and happy and want to be left alone, or when they're struggling and can figure it out on their own, as opposed to when they actually need our help. This sort of thoughtful responsiveness requires us to slow down, get out of our own heads, and remember that a strong relationship isn't about unwavering connection. It's about noticing what your child needs at this moment, what you need, letting your kids deal as often as they can, and taking care of yourself as often as you can.

Taking space is also crucial for you. Making time for your BuRPs will help you stay more present and patient when you're with your children again. Yes, there will always be times when it's not possible to physically remove yourself from the situation, either because you didn't have the foresight or money to book a babysitter, or you're stuck in a hotel room during a rainy family trip to Orlando. When that happens, you need to find a way to get a little headspace. The ability to not get caught up in our kids' psychological and emotional storms is a powerful way to keep family drama to a minimum.

Don't freak out. I'm not saying you should never hang out with your children. Of course not. I'm just saying that most modern parents—even those of us who work full-time—tend to err so far in the direction of constant engagement that we have a little wiggle room to play with without worrying about damaging our relationship with our children. You might decide to get some space from your kids whenever you notice you've been on edge for several days, but it can also be an intentional decision to swap weekend afternoons with your parenting partner or friend so you each get some time off on a regular basis. Whatever way it works out for you, the trick is to enjoy it. Try not to spend the whole time worrying about your kids or the mortgage or whether your hair is thinning. The whole point of getting away is to calm yourself down, not work yourself into a lather before you even get back home.

WHAT TO DO WHEN YOU'RE NOT SPENDING ENOUGH TIME WITH YOUR KIDS

WHILE MANY PARENTS don't get enough space from their kids, the opposite is true for some folks. Not spending enough time with your kids can lead to feelings of shame, confusion, regret, or guilt, all of which are major triggers. Perhaps you're not with your children more because of long hours at work, military deployment, divorce, or physical or mental-health issues. Whatever the reason, it will likely include a host of triggers, from the stress of long work days, the trauma of combat, or the logistical and emotional challenges of ending a relationship and coparenting with an ex. As we've previously discussed, all of these triggers can impact your parenting, even if they don't seem directly connected.

If you feel guilty about not see-ing the kids more, you may feel extra pressure to make each moment per-fect, and doubly guilty if you lose your shit during what precious little time you have with them. We'll talk more later about what to do when you feel like you're about to explode, but in the meanwhile, remember this: These are all real issues, and they're common among folks who aren't with their kids on a regular basis. You are definitely not alone.

If you have some control over your schedule, do what you can to get more time with them. If you don't, connect with your children however you can; FaceTime is a great option with little ones, and text messages work well with older children. Physical letters can be especially meaningful; children love receiving mail, and they can reread those letters each time they need to feel connected to you. And don't forget to practice your BuRPs when you're not with them; that self-care will help you be as calm, present, and con-nected as possible when you are with your kids.

What I'm asking you to do—throughout this book, and especially in this chapter—requires a fundamental shift in your approach to yourself and your parenting. It's about creating new habits and routines, finding a new balance, and trusting that when you give your kids more space, they will step up to the challenge.

How to Get Actual Space Away from Your Kids

While it is possible to be physically near your children and not pay attention to them, it's not easy. They clamor for our attention, and even when they're not actually seeking us out, their shenanigans distract us. Either way, it's highly unlikely that you will get the headspace you need unless you actually get out of the house (or kick the kids out; either works). Here are some strategies to get you started:

★ **Let other people take care of your children.** Think babysitters, grandparents, aunts and uncles, best friends, older siblings, childcare providers, and preschool teachers. As long as you trust them, it's all good. If you can't afford help, start or join a babysitting co-op and take turns caring for one another's kids.

★ **Drop them off at playdates, and let other parents do the same at your house.** For a variety of reasons, the era of kids coming home from school and scampering off with the neighborhood kids until dinner time has passed. (Sob.) These days we schedule playdates. Playdates are fantastic, but unless you enjoy spending time with the other parents (which is great when it works out!), set the precedent early that playdates are *drop-off*. Confirm this plan ahead of time with the other parent so everyone understands the expectations, and each time your kid is the guest, offer to host in return.

★ **Drop them off at practices.** There is no need to sit on the sidelines unless you enjoy it or want to connect with your community. (If it's the latter, grab a chair and a cup of coffee and proceed to pay zero attention to your children. Don't comment, praise, or encourage. Catch up with your friends instead.) If you need to connect with your crew, stay for ten minutes and then go. Otherwise, check in with the coach or instructor and hit the road. Go for a walk, run some errands, or just enjoy a little quiet time in your car.

★ **Carpool. Carpool. Carpool.** The work required to set one up is well worth the payoff of not always having to drive.

★ **Accept the help.** I can't tell you how many times I've heard parents refuse sincere offers of help. I've done it myself, for a variety of reasons that I can no longer recall but clearly seemed reasonable at the time. Don't do this. If someone you trust offers to take your children for an hour or a day or a weekend, *accept the help*.

How to Get Headspace Even When You're with Your Kids

. . . .

As much as you may try to get some space from your children, it won't always be possible or desirable. You're going to be with them, and you want that time to be as enjoyable as possible. But just because you're physically near your kids doesn't mean you need to engage with them at every single moment. The ability to consciously decide whether or not to step into the fray is a powerful step toward keeping your shit together. Here are a few strategies for getting a little headspace when you're all together.

★ **Either pay attention to your children or ignore them.** As you've heard me say more than once, multitasking when you're with your kids is frustrating for them and stressful for you, and makes it way more likely you'll explode. If you want or need to do something without the kids, get them involved with a toy, book, or game, and then *leave them alone.* Do your work, read your book, or cook a meal, and resist the temptation to comment on or question them about what they're doing. When you're ready to reengage (or it becomes clear that they need you), then close your computer, put away your phone, and get your parenting game on. If you have babies and toddlers at home, start training them now. You'd be surprised how long little ones can entertain themselves with a few blocks or balls given the chance.

★ **Let them wait.** This sounds obvious, but it's something many parents struggle with. If you're cooking dinner or paying bills or talking on the phone and a child appears with a question or request, don't try to handle both things at once. Instead, say something like, "Please wait, I'll be with you in a second." They almost certainly won't hear you the first time, so feel free to repeat fifteen times. They may be annoyed, but they'll adapt, and they'll definitely survive. Learning to be patient and wait for your turn is a major life skill, so get 'em going early.

★ **Don't give a happy child ice cream.** This is one of my favorite pieces of parenting advice, and it comes from the actor Jack Black. If your child is happy, leave well enough alone. Don't get involved in their game or homework or sandcastle or whatever they're doing. Resist the urge to praise, ask questions, or offer them help. Enjoy the opportunity for a little downtime; they'll need you soon enough.

★ **Tolerate your children's boredom so they can learn to do the same.** Being bored is part of life, so your kids might as well learn how to deal with it now. Their boredom is not your problem to solve, and the more energy you expend trying to entertain them, the more stressed or annoyed you're going to become, and we both know how that's going to end. Here are some possible responses to the dreaded phrase "I'm bored":

"Thanks for the update!"

"If you need something to do, you can always clean your room / take out the garbage / feed the dog / [insert chore of choice here]."

"I know you'll figure something out."

"I'm Mom/Dad. Nice to meet you!"

★ **Let them figure it out on their own.** Tending to each and every one of your kids' requests will wear you down. It's even more exhausting if you've got a kid who asks for help the instant things get even slightly hard. Resist the urge to jump right in; instead mumble something about being right there, honey, and give them a couple of minutes to struggle. You'd be surprised at how often they can open the jar or tie their shoes or find their favorite doll on their own when you give them a minute.

★ **Resist the urge to referee every fight.** Whether it's another sibling spat or a bicker session between friends, take a breath before you get involved. Not all disagreements require parental involvement, especially if you're already triggered for any reason. Yes, you will want to give your kids skills and strategies to resolve conflicts, but you also need to give them the space to figure it out themselves.

★ **Try not to take your kid's crap personally.** This can be tough because there are few things in life that feel quite as personal as our own offspring. Even if your toddler is looking right at you as they fling their green beans to the floor, even when your teen screams they hate you with a vigor you never could have imagined, remember that *it's not about you*. Your children's behavior is more about whatever is going on in their still-developing brains than it is about you. Keeping a little perspective on the situation will go a long way toward keeping calm. Breathe in, breathe out, and let it go.

★ **Do not get into a power struggle.** Say yes when you can, say no when you need to, and then Do Not Engage. Ignore the nagging and whining. Don't get sucked into negotiations, and don't pay any attention to the insults or threats. Stick your fingers in your ears if you have to. If they come to you with a calm, reasonable argument, then you can change your mind if you want to. Otherwise, your go-to response is "You asked and I answered," which can be shortened to "Asked and answered." The sooner your kids realize they're not going to get anywhere with their shenanigans, they'll cut way back on the BS.

★ **Pretend they're someone else's kid.** Other people's kids are adorable (most of the time). This isn't necessarily because they're cuter or better behaved than ours, it's because it's easier to keep a little distance and perspective when we're not responsible for them. Their antics aren't our fault, their behavior isn't reflective of our parenting or linked to our sense of success and failure. Their fingers don't fit our buttons. If you can pretend your kids are someone else's, then their behavior is way, way less likely to push yours.

★ **Don't take responsibility for their happiness.** It is *not* your job to make your child happy. It is your job to keep them as safe as possible, and to help them mature and grow into reasonably functional adults. A big part of that is learning how to experience and deal with a variety of emotions, including the shitty ones. Letting your kids feel their feelings without getting caught up in them or needing to fix them is an effective way to get a little headspace from their chaos. Stay with your children and offer comfort if they need you, but remember that there's nothing wrong with feeling bad, and it will pass.

★ **Remember this mantra:** They may be my monkeys, but this still ain't my circus.

Hopefully by now I've convinced you that devoting a little less time and energy to your children can be a good thing, both for their development and your ability to keep your shit together when you are with them. Between your newfound freedom and your growing commitment to your BuRPs, you should be well on your way to dramatically reducing the likelihood that you'll lose your shit. Even so, it's still going to happen, which is why the book doesn't end here.

CHAPTER 8

What You've Been Waiting For: How, Exactly, to Not Lose Your Shit

NOTICE

★

PAUSE

★

DO LITERALLY ANYTHING ELSE

Finally. We're here.

Over the course of the book, we've explored what your meltdowns look like, what causes them, and how to prevent them. We talked about your brain and nervous system, and the ways in which your buttons get bigger, brighter, and more sensitive when you're triggered. We've reviewed the range of events and experiences that can trigger you, and you understand how they can make you vulnerable to your kids' shenanigans. You've got a bunch of BuRPs (strategies) for keeping your buttons as small and dark as possible, and hopefully I've convinced you that getting a little space from your kiddo is good for both of you.

All of this business about buttons and triggers has been in the service of preventing meltdowns whenever possible. Yet you will still find yourself on the verge of, or neck deep in, an explosion from time to time. What can I say? Shit still happens.

Of course it does.

It happens when I'm awakened at 2 a.m. by a screaming kid or a barfing cat or my own damn thoughts, and I can't go back to sleep and the next day I'm just too tired to deal. It happens when a friend gets a terrible diagnosis or a potential book deal falls through or I get rear-ended. It happens because old neuronal habits die really hard. It's like freaking out at my kids is my native language, and even though I've worked my butt off to learn a new one, I slip back into it from time to time. It happens because sometimes life crises overpower all of my coping skills, and even with all of the support and self-compassion I can muster, I'm still lit up brighter than a Christmas tree. And it happens because sometimes my daughters find a brand-new button, one that none of us knew existed, and they push and they push and, well, there I am again, standing in the kitchen, hands spread flat on the counter, breathing and breathing and trying my damnedest not to lose it.

Likely the same will be true for you. Fortunately, you're ready to make a change. Things are going to be different next time because, at the risk of sounding a bit crass, you're ready to stop FARTing all over your kids. (Sadly, it's unlikely they'll offer you the same courtesy anytime soon.) Remember, FARTing is about strong Feelings, Automatic Reactions, and Toxic behaviors. The next time you feel like you're losing it, just put down your phone, offload the children, and spend thirty minutes sweating on the elliptical instead.

Oh, if only it were so easy.

As you and I and every single parent on the planet knows, while the BuRP strategies in this book are simple, they're not always easy. It can be incredibly hard to find the time, space, energy, and support to take care of yourself, especially if you haven't been in the habit of doing so. Having said that, your BuRPs are worth your limited time and energy because they will make it (a) less likely that you'll be triggered in the first place and (b) more likely that you'll notice when you

> You will still find yourself on the verge of, or neck deep in, an explosion from time to time.

are triggered, so you can pause, chill out a little bit, and choose to do something, anything other than losing your shit.

And that, dear reader, is your *numero uno* strategy when you find yourself losing your shit with your kids: Notice, Pause, and Do Literally Anything Else.

It's not fancy or complicated, which is good because you don't need fancy or complicated. You need feasible and effective. You need something you can actually do when you don't know what else to do. And you can do this.

There are a million parenting moves that don't involve losing it with your kids, and folks often get hung up on picking the Best Possible Choice. Good news: Anything that's better than freaking out is the Best Possible Choice for Now. Doing something else is the easy part. Getting yourself into the right headspace to do something else is the hard part, so we're going to make it as easy as possible. It's all about noticing, pausing, and doing literally anything else, so let's dig into it.

Noticing

N oticing is your superpower. At the end of the day, in the heat of the moment, when you're down to the wire, noticing is your go-to move. If you don't notice that you're about to flip out, you can't make a choice not to. If you don't notice that you're mid-scream, you can't decide to shut your mouth. Noticing is about self-awareness, and self-awareness is clutch.

This practice is powerful in its simplicity, but it's not easy. Don't get me wrong; it's not hard to notice the sunset blazing across the horizon while you relax on the beach and the kids play happily on the sand. It's easy to notice the words on the page of a particularly interesting magazine article. It's easy to be aware of what's going on inside us and around us when we're doing one thing at a time and we're not triggered and our prefrontal cortexes (the noticing centers of our brains) are fully powered and running the show.

Noticing is about self-awareness, and self-awareness is clutch.

It's also easy to notice a screaming kid or a buzzing phone but that's not actually noticing, that's reacting. If you want to be all picky about it, we could call it reactive noticing. Some external stimulus yanks your attention away, likely triggering you in the process. That sort of reactive noticing / attention yanking scenario is how most of us spend most of our waking time. It's the secret villain of shit loss, and we need to do whatever we can to combat it. Single-tasking is a great place to start.

The minute we get triggered, our brains amp up the Fight, Flight, Freeze, or Freak Out reaction. Our limbic systems (our inner toddlers) fire up and our prefrontal cortexes (the grown-up in our brains) shut down. Our nervous systems prepare us to move quickly, even in response to emotional and psychological threats that don't require a physical response. And so there we are, all agitated and twitchy and ready to leap into action but with nowhere to go. Whether we realize it or not, we've gone from noticing mode to reacting mode, buttons are primed and ready for pushing. The minute kiddo #1 starts tossing sand at #2, we have the action our nervous system has been looking for, and so we leap, and shit is lost.

HOW TO NOTICE WHEN YOU'RE ABOUT TO LOSE IT

The point of noticing is to catch yourself in tense moments. Ideally, you'll realize you're about to lose it before you actually do, but the truth is you can stop yourself at any point in a meltdown, even mid-freak-out. Most explosions actually happen in stages; neuroscientist and author Dan Siegel describes them as Trigger, Transition, Immersion, and Recovery.

STAGE 1: TRIGGER. Something triggers you. It could be a day spent being inadvertently touched by too many people at a hot amusement park, the anniversary of your father's death, news of a natural disaster, or an offhand comment from another parent on the playground after school. You may be epically triggered or barely triggered. You might be triggered for a few minutes or hours, or your buttons may have been on high alert for years now. You may be aware that you're a walking button, just waiting to be pushed, or you may have no idea. Regardless of the details, you're triggered.

Paying attention to your tells (as we discussed in Chapter 3) will help you recognize when you're triggered. We all have particular ways in which our minds and bodies behave when our buttons are lighting up. It may be certain thoughts that pop up when you're anxious or that pain in your shoulder starts throbbing every time you're stressed. It could be a tone of voice you notice yourself using; I respond to my daughters with short, clipped sentences, and by the time I'm reduced to "OK" in response to everything they say, I'm about three seconds away from a shit loss. Everyone's tells are different, and yours may be completely bizarre, but don't worry about it. You don't need to change them or fix them; just learn them and respect them.

STAGE 2: TRANSITION. At some point, your button is pushed, most likely by your child. This is the beginning of the transition stage, when you're moving from Not Losing Your Shit to Losing Your Shit. This is when your nervous system is amped up, just looking for a reason to Fight, Flee, Freeze, or Freak Out. You might feel slightly twitchy, or you may be jumping out of your skin. Several factors can influence how long you stay in the transition phase, including how triggered you are, how hard and fast your buttons are being pushed, and what you're doing in response. You might go from zero to meltdown in a matter of seconds, but if you can notice that your buttons are being pushed and remember to breathe or step outside or sing your favorite Springsteen song, you may never make it to the Immersion stage, which is a good thing.

STAGE 3: IMMERSION. This is just a fancy word for Losing Your Shit. It's a good word for it because being immersed in something is pretty much the opposite of noticing. Your nervous system is in full-on freak-out mode and you're FARTing all over the place. You're overwhelmed by Big Feelings, you're reacting automatically, and your behavior is toxic. Even though you know that screaming and slamming and throwing remote controls is making things worse, once you get going, it's hard to stop. This is because your adulting brain (PFC) has gone offline, and the toddler (limbic system) is running the show. And as we all know, toddlers make poor life choices.

STAGE 4: RECOVERY. Eventually, you'll wear yourself out or your parenting partner will gently suggest that perhaps you need a break (at which point you will likely bite their head off before stomping out of the room) or you'll see the terrified tears streaming down your child's face and your guilt and shame will shut you down. This is the beginning of the recovery phase, which, under the best of circumstances, is when you pull your shit together and reconnect with your kiddo. This is a tricky time, as your buttons will still be very vulnerable, meaning you might pull it together or you might explode all over again. We'll talk more in Chapter 9 about what to do during the recovery phase so you won't lose your shit again.

HOW TO GET BETTER
AT NOTICING

Noticing is the key to interrupting this cycle. *Noticing is about waking up to whatever's happening.* You may have had moments when you realized you were about to epically explode at your kids, and you managed to do something else instead. The problem is that it can all feel so unpredictable; some days we have our shit together and other days we're losing it and we never know which day we're gonna get. That's par for the course when it comes to our kids and their half-baked brains, but it's no good for us.

Far too many people spend their entire lives at the mercy of whatever happens to grab their attention, never realizing that they have the ability to *not* take the bait. Each time we notice that we've been distracted, stuck in a repetitive thought cycle, or flooded by emotions, we can choose to step back and watch the show, rather than stepping into the lead role.

Noticing is *always* an option. Sometimes you notice something significant, like the angry words flying out of your mouth, but it's worth noticing seemingly minor moments as well. If you often walk around with a tense jaw, try to notice when that happens, and loosen it. Adding up enough of those small shifts in your awareness and behavior can make your day significantly easier.

Practicing your BuRPs will make it more likely that you'll check yourself before you wreck yourself. When you're not exhausted or immersed in your phone, you'll be more likely to be aware of what you're doing. And the first step toward practicing gratitude is realizing just how pissy and ungrateful you currently feel. You can't choose to slow down if you don't notice how fast you're moving.

Just as with any skill, the key to getting better at noticing is practice. Practice noticing like your sanity depends on it, because, well, it does. The more often you step back and get some perspective, the stronger your noticing muscles will become. The neuronal connections in your brain that help you notice will grow stronger, smoother, and more connected each time you activate them. Eventually, your brain will default to noticing before you even realize it.

Here's an example: The other day I was stuck in traffic and running late for a meeting. I noticed that I was becoming increasingly irritable, so I tried to let go of my cranky

> Far too many people spend their entire lives at the mercy of whatever happens to grab their attention, never realizing that they have the ability to not take the bait.

thoughts, but I couldn't. They kept coming back. I needed something immediate and concrete to focus on. I picked something easy: the brake lights, the round red circles of light lined up in front of me.

Getting out of my own head—if only for a moment—and grounding my attention in something outside of my thoughts helped me notice that I was sitting right in front of the building where my meeting was happening. I was so busy being pissed off about the traffic that I almost missed my turn.

Although noticing is a crucial step toward calming down, don't wait for those stressful moments to start practicing. Those are crises, and it's incredibly difficult (if not impossible) for our brains to learn something new in the midst of a crisis. Start when it's easy, when you're not dealing with strong emotions or confusing thoughts or psychotic toddlers. Practice noticing when you're lying in bed, sipping your coffee, or sitting in the car for two minutes after school drop-off. The more often you notice when it's easy, the easier it will be to do when it's hard.

> Start when it's easy. Practice noticing when you're lying in bed, sipping your coffee, or sitting in the car for two minutes after school drop-off.

WHAT TO NOTICE WHEN YOU'RE NOT SURE WHAT TO NOTICE

While it is true that you can intentionally notice anything, the options can feel overwhelming, so I'll narrow them down for you. Try to notice something that is actually happening in the present moment, preferably something that isn't triggering. If you're anywhere in the transition or immersion phases, focus on anything you can see, feel, taste, hear, or smell. Getting yourself out of your brain and connected to the physical world will calm you down. If you're triggered, or trying to get some insights into your triggers, your best bet is to notice your thoughts, feelings, bodily sensations, or behaviors. Here are a few suggestions to get you started:

★ **Notice your thoughts.** What are you thinking about? Are you freaking out about a work deadline? Are you worried about your child's relentless cough? Are you obsessively replaying a shitty interaction with a friend? You don't need to find answers or fix anything; the goal here is to realize that you're thinking, and that you can choose whether or not you want to continue doing so.

★ **Notice your feelings.** How are you feeling? Stressed? Scared? Anxious? Rageful? No matter how intense or unpleasant your feelings are, do your best to remember that feelings don't last forever. They all have a beginning, a middle, and an end, and you just need to hang in there until they pass. In addition, every feeling is OK (really, I promise!), but not every behavior is OK, and noticing what you're feeling is the first step toward not reacting thoughtlessly.

★ **Notice what's happening in your body.** Are you wearing your shoulders like earrings? Is your back tighter than a rubber band on the verge of snapping? Are you in pain? Is your head throbbing? You might be able to shift your position, drop your shoulders, do a quick stretch, or pop some ibuprofen. Or there might not be a damn thing you can do about it, but if you don't notice what's happening in your body in the first place, you won't be able to address what's bothering you. You'll just be tense and in pain, triggered up and ready to blow.

★ **Notice what you're doing.** It's crazy to think we could do something without being aware of it, but our brains shift into autopilot whenever they can in order to preserve resources and energy. Imagine if we had to consciously think through each motion required just to walk up a flight of steps. It would take forever, and we'd be exhausted by the time we got to the top. This is why we're able to pull into the parking lot at work with absolutely no recollection of driving there. That's a potentially bad thing when you're doing more than one thing at a time and getting increasingly stressed by all of it. So just take a minute and notice what you're doing.

★ **Notice your breath.** If you're so worked up that you can't remember what you're supposed to notice, just breathe. Breathing, and noticing your breathing, is an easy and effective way to get a little space from the chaos. Slow down your breath or count your inhales and exhales or take three deep breaths. Just breathe.

One more note: There's a reason why so many of us work so hard to distract ourselves from whatever is happening. Sometimes reality bites and the present moment sucks. Our thoughts seem crazy, our feelings are scary, our body isn't what it used to be, and life is hard. It's just not fun. Just let it be OK. Don't feel the need to fix

ADVANCED NOTICING
(AKA MEDITATION)

LOTS OF FOLKS think that meditation is about clearing your mind or keeping your attention perfectly focused for as long as possible. Wrongo. For the purposes of this book, you can think of it as Advanced Noticing Practice. Just like going to the gym strengthens your muscles, meditating strengthens the noticing part of your brain.

Here's how to do it:

1. Find someplace quiet and comfortable where you will have a decent chance of being left alone for two to twenty minutes. Sit down, set your phone to Do Not Disturb, and start a timer.

2. Pick something to focus on. Lots of folks pick their breath, but you can go with whatever works for you. Repeat a prayer or mantra, observe the trees around you, listen to the sounds you can hear, or count backward from one hundred.

3. Notice when your mind wanders. Notice that I didn't say "if," I said "when." Within a few seconds, your thoughts will wander. They might stay close, or they might head straight into some crappy memories, confusing ideas, intense cravings, or unhelpful images. Don't get caught up in all that brain activity. There's no need to explore, question, or judge your thoughts. Don't worry about how far your mind went or how long it was gone for. Just notice that it wandered.

4. Go back to the thing you were focusing on in the first place: your breath, prayer, or counting. Pick up where you left off or start again.

5. Repeat.

6. Repeat again and again until your timer dings.

7. Do it again the next day. And the day after that.

If you notice that your brain has wandered sixty times in sixty seconds, you haven't failed at meditation. You've completed sixty noticing reps, you've practiced sixty more times. This is exactly what you were going for. Well done!

things or rush into the next step. Try not to get all judgy or frustrated with yourself. Those sorts of reactions are unnecessary and counter-productive; they're more likely to tense you up than calm you down. Whatever it is will pass. In the meanwhile, try a little self-compassion, and do whatever you can to make it easier to notice going forward.

Doing just one thing at a time makes it easier to notice whatever is happening in and around you.

There's no shortcut to notic-ing; either you're aware of what's going on in and around you, or you're swirling in the chaos. However, there are a few hacks that can make it eas-ier and more likely that you'll realize when you've gotten lost in your own thoughts. Slowing down is a great place to start; it's not impossible to notice when you're rushing, but it is more challenging. Turning down the noise can help too. Background noise—whether it's from the radio or TV or something else—is dis-tracting. Doing just one thing at a time makes it easier to notice whatever is happening in and around you. If your mind is especially distractible, keep it focused by narrating your experience.

Finally, physical reminders can make it easier to notice. Anything that brings your attention back to the present moment will work. Keep a smooth stone in your pocket; the physical sensation of holding it can give you something to focus your attention on. Wear a beaded bracelet (sometimes called a *mala*) as a reminder to breathe. Write your favorite BuRPs on a sticky note, or keep a list of things to notice on your refrigerator. Hang religious or spiritual images, paintings, or pictures that make you happy in areas where you are most likely to struggle with noticing. (One of my friends taped a photo of her kids in a happy, calm moment on the inside of her kitchen cabinet, so she could look at it whenever she felt like strangling them.)

You can notice what's happening at any point in the process, and as soon as you do, you're ready to pause. Noticing and pausing are easiest to do during the trigger and transition phases; when you can wake up and realize that your buttons are huge and super pushable or that they're actively being pushed and you're teetering on the edge of a massive meltdown, you can choose to do anything other than freak out. It's also possible to stop yourself mid-shitstorm, but it can feel a bit tricky until you get the hang of it. Keep practicing. It will get easier.

Pausing

I f noticing is a shift in your awareness, then pausing is a shift in your behavior. In fact, it's the first crucial step toward staying calm. It's exactly as simple as it sounds; just take a brief break from whatever you're doing

There's a reason I'm suggesting you pause instead of stop. Stopping feels big and hard and permanent. Pausing is gentler and easier; it's just a bathroom break during a movie, a time-out in the middle of an intense game. A pause is temporary. You're not totally bailing on the moment; you're still going to have a talk about why it's not appropriate to leave snotty tissues all over the house or shove Play-Doh in the headphone jack of their sibling's phone. You're just going to do it after you've had a chance to get your shit together.

The pause can be as brief or as lengthy as you want. Super-intense, emotional, or complex moments require a longer pause. The closer you are to the immersion phase of a meltdown, the more time you may need to pause. Fortunately, the more you practice the pause, the better you'll get at it and the less time you'll need for it.

> The pause can be as brief or as lengthy as you want. Super-intense, emotional, or complex moments require a longer pause.

One more important point: When you're in the midst of the pause, *you don't know what will happen next*. This can be challenging for the control freaks among us, but it's actually a good thing. The pause isn't about scrambling for a solution or plotting your revenge. If you're doing that, you haven't really paused the crazy train you're on; you've just switched tracks. Your buttons are still as activated as ever. Even if it seems like you're no longer losing it, you're actually gearing up for round two.

The pause isn't about a plan; it's about activating your parasympathetic nervous system (which calms down your buttons) and giving yourself a little time and space to calm those buttons down. Walk to the other side of the room, take a deep breath, put your hands flat on the kitchen counter and trace your fingers. Do whatever it takes to stay in the pause, because that's where you're going to find the answer to the eternal parenting question: *What the hell do I do now?*

The answer is simple: Literally Anything Else.

Doing Literally Anything Else

. . . .

O nce you've noticed that you're on the fast train to freak-out town and have hit pause on the moment, then all you have to do is, well, anything else. The purpose of the anything else is to (a) calm you down, (b) diffuse the moment, and (c) redirect the tense energy that's building up. You can do all of this directly by taking some deep breaths, praying, or getting quiet; or indirectly by redirecting all that triggered energy into anything other than exploding. There is no right or wrong here; the trick is to find something that works for you and your family, and by *works* I mean "helps you not lose your shit."

Here are a few things to keep in mind as you figure out what works and what doesn't:

★ **You're always practicing something, even if it's something you don't necessarily want to get better at.** For example, if you're trying to yell less, then don't go scream into a pillow. While it's true that exploding in your bed is better than exploding at your child, any form of yelling probably isn't a great practice, as it may increase the likelihood that you'll revert to yelling the next time you're ready to let loose.

★ **Don't choose something that is likely to trigger you.** You might be inclined to reach for a bottle of wine or your smartphone but either one is likely to light you up, so instead of actually calming down, you're just prolonging the trigger phase. If you're not sure what to do instead, review your BuRPs; many of them will work in a tight moment.

★ **Do the best you can with what you have.** This is not about perfection. It's just about not losing your shit.

YEAH, YEAH—BUT WHAT EXACTLY AM I SUPPOSED TO DO?

As soon as you wake up and realize that you're anywhere in the midst of losing it, just pause for as long as you need to come up with something else. As long as it's something you want to be practicing and it doesn't trigger you further, you're good to go. However, it can be hard to come up with new ideas in a moment of crisis, so here are some suggestions to consider; feel free to use them or come up with your own.

★ **Breathe.** I know I'm being a bit naggy about this whole breathing thing, but it really does work. Also, you can't breathe and scream at the same time, so that's cool.

★ **Step away.** As long as the child is somewhere safe, you can walk away. Even if she's throwing a massive tantrum, better that you take some space than get in her face. Remember that night when I put my girls in front of the TV because that was the only thing I could think to do instead of yelling at them? Well, that worked too. Do the best you can with what you have, and do what you can to get some space when you need it.

★ **Stay silent.** If you're fairly certain that nothing good is going to come out of your mouth, well, then, shut it. If you really can't control yourself, put your hand over your mouth. At least then your angry words will be muffled, which isn't nearly as toxic sounding.

★ **Simplify your thoughts.** Whenever you notice that your brain is full of irritable thoughts about your kids or parenting partner or whomever, do what you can to get some space from them. Simplifying your thoughts will help you calm down; I have offered a number of strategies for doing so in Chapter 6.

★ **Stretch or move.** Your nervous system is all amped up and ready for action, so why not jump into action, literally? Do some jumping jacks. Hop on one foot. Get your downward dog on. Walk up and down the stairs twenty-seven times. Now that my girls are older, I've been known to run around the outside of the house and come back in. (I tell them that I need some fresh air to calm down and that I'll be right back and they had better not follow me if they know what's good for them.)

★ **Put your hands flat on the counter** or feel your feet on the floor. Putting your skin in contact with a hard surface can help you feel more grounded and calm.

★ **Talk it out**, but not too much. Telling your kids what's about to happen is a great way to diffuse the tension. Try

> If you're fairly certain that nothing good is going to come out of your mouth, well, then, shut it.

something like, "I'm feeling pretty stressed, and I'm about to snap at you. I need to calm down. You can breathe quietly with me, but if you nag or whine at me, I will probably bite your head off." (You're welcome to use my exact words, in which case you may want to explain to your kids that you won't literally bite their heads off. I made that mistake once and it totally freaked them out.) Again, you're not going to undermine yourself; you're actually modeling a behavior that would be great for them to utilize sometime.

★ **Repeat your safe word (some people call it a mantra).** Some folks get their mantras from a guru or other spiritual guide, but you can also just pick one that you like. It doesn't matter what the word is, or if it's even a real word, or where it comes from, as long as it helps you calm down and doesn't trigger you further. For example, you could choose "Let It Go" or "Hakuna Matata" unless anything Disney-related makes your blood boil. (My current mantra is "Shama Lama Ding Dong," from the Otis Day and the Knights song in *Animal House*.)

★ **Turn on some tunes and shake your groove thing.** Sing really freaking loud if you have to.

★ **Get silly.** Unfortunately, humor is one of the most underutilized tricks up our parenting sleeves, perhaps because some folks are worried about undermining their own authority. This isn't going to happen. Instead, you'll be modeling an effective response to difficult moments. You might even crack your kids up, which could help you reconnect more quickly. So, go ahead. Crack a joke. Make a face. Strike a pose. Sing a terrible aria. Wiggle like a worm. I frequently open my mouth to shout and end up squeaking or singing or babbling nonsense or throwing my hands in the air like I just don't care. If I really need to yell, "AY, CARAMBA" works well, except it often reminds me that my daughters have never watched *The Simpsons*, which strikes me as a major parenting fail. Sigh.

One note about humor as an Anything Else strategy: Be careful with sarcasm. This is not the time to mock, tease, needle, or generally poke fun at your kids. Those sorts of reactions are often misunderstood in tense moments, and are likely to make things worse.

★ **Send a little love your way.** Cut yourself some slack and practice some self-compassion. Remind yourself that parenting is hard and that it's OK that it's hard. Remember that you're not the only parent to lose their shit at their kids, and that you don't have to be perfect.

★ **Make a list of your favorite Anything Else strategies.** Put the list on the fridge or the bathroom mirror or the dashboard of your car or write it backward and tape it to your forehead. This will be helpful when you are just aware enough to notice that you're losing it, but your grip on reality is too tenuous to remember all of the things you could be doing instead.

Notice, Pause, and Do Literally Anything Else. That's all it takes to not lose your shit with your kids. It's simple, but not easy. Fortunately, it gets way easier with practice. And you must keep practicing. Don't give up if you feel like it doesn't work the first two or twelve times you try. It's like learning to walk or speak a new language. Falling on your face and stumbling over your words are part of the process, not a reason to give up.

Even so, shit will still be lost. It will happen. It will happen less often and less intensely, but it will happen. This is such a common dynamic that parenting experts have come up with a handy little phrase for it: *Rupture, Repair, Repeat*. How you handle the aftermath of an explosion has a lot to do with how likely you will be to repeat it. You can emerge from your meltdown fully triggered, buttons ready to be pushed, or you can come out the other side significantly chiller and way less likely to lose it again. Chill is good, so let's focus on that.

CHAPTER 9

After the Shitstorm Has Passed

BE KIND

★

GET CURIOUS

★

MAKE NICE WITH YOUR KIDS

So you've lost your shit. Now what?

The details vary, but most parents revert to one of three different reactions after the shitstorm has passed. Some beat themselves up for exploding again, and stew in their own guilt and shame. You know the script; it's some version of "I'm a terrible parent, and I'm failing at the most important work of my life. I suck at this and my kids will never be happy, functional adults."

Other parents become overly effusive toward their children in an attempt to reconnect. They may apologize profusely, or offer an additional fifteen minutes of screen time or extra dessert, without ever talking about what happened and why it happened.

Finally, some parents get all JADED, and I don't just mean burnt out and cynical. This clever acronym, which I totally did not make up, stands for Justify, Argue, Defend, Explain, or Dismiss. This is an internal process designed to rationalize the explosion: Your screaming wasn't *that* bad and your kid *was* being a total punk and your spouse's flight *was* canceled and you had a totally weird interaction with your BFF that you can't quite figure out and your knee is acting up and the kid really was being exceptionally awful and yadda yadda yadda. Besides, the dishwasher needs to be unloaded and you need to get dinner in the oven and nobody's freaking out right now so you might as well just get on with the day, right?

Admittedly, these sorts of responses aren't necessarily wrong. Kids *can* be total punks. We parents often have legitimate reasons to be stressed and overwhelmed. The damn dishwasher *does* need to be unloaded, and a sweet treat isn't the worst thing in the world, is it? Of course not, but all of that is beside the point. The point is that these aren't the most skillful ways to respond to your meltdowns, for a few different reasons.

Self-flagellation feels awful, and it puts you in an even worse mood than you were in before. Shame is an emotional dead end. It leaves you feeling stuck and unsure of where to go next. It's a major trigger, putting you at risk of repeating the same shitty behaviors you were beating yourself up for in the first place. Similarly, getting all JADED doesn't offer any insights into what happened or what to do differently next time. It just wears you down, and that sort of emotional sparring is, yup, you guessed it: another trigger.

Sweeping your explosions under the rug might help you calm down in the moment, but again, there's no healing or growth or change. To make matters even worse, whatever you try to do to distract yourself (smartphone, chocolate, wine, etc.) may actually trigger you more.

And sadly, spoiling your kid won't make it easier to spare the rod the next time you're ready to explode. It might make both of you feel better in the short term, but as years of experience have shown me, there aren't any solutions or strategies buried in the bottom of that hot fudge sundae.

While I was writing this chapter, I posted a picture on social media with an image of my

> We parents often have legitimate reasons to be stressed and overwhelmed.

computer screen with the words "After the Shitstorm" on it. A few folks shared that they always apologize to their kids after they lose it. (More on this in a bit.) Another friend commented that perhaps we should put away our shit umbrellas. I laughed out loud, because oh good lord what a disgusting image. And then I realized that it's not an entirely inaccurate one. The shitstorm is over, but when we beat ourselves up or get all JADED and frustrated, it's as though we're still standing under a shit umbrella, all triggered and agitated as we get shat upon even more. Yuck.

So how about we close up those shit umbrellas and try something different?

After the Storm Has Passed

Y ou might think I'm about to give you a bunch of suggestions for how to reconnect with your kids after you freak out all over them. *Au contraire, mon frère.* In the same way that preventing a meltdown isn't about your kids, recovering from one isn't about them either. It's about you and your triggers and your buttons, so that's where we're gonna start.

The first step is to calm down. This is nonnegotiable. Your body has been flooded with stress hormones, and it takes time for your parasympathetic nervous system to kick in, shut down the power to your buttons, and get your adulting brain back in the game. If you rush into reconnection while you're still triggered, there's a good chance your buttons will be pushed yet again and you'll end up snapping instead of snuggling. As long as your child is safe, strap on your oxygen mask and take care of yourself first.

There are a ton of ways to calm yourself down. Breathing, stretching, stepping away, and simplifying your thoughts will help put the brakes on the speeding train in your brain and body. Whatever is on your Anything Else list will also help. Experiment with a few things, and you'll figure out what works for you. In addition, I've got two simple strategies that will definitely do the trick: self-compassion and curiosity. Not only are these inherently more pleasant than berating yourself, but they're also more effective.

SELF-COMPASSION
Kindness Is More Powerful Than You Realize

We explored self-compassion in Chapter 5, and hopefully you've been standing in front of the mirror and talking to yourself in your best Stuart Smalley voice. (Joking!) Seriously, though, I hope you have been practicing treating yourself with a lot more kindness whenever possible. And if you haven't gotten that far, maybe you've started noticing when you mentally berate yourself? Noticing is the first step. Once you realize that you're treating yourself like crap, you can make a different choice, a choice to remember that:

★ Parenting is hard for everyone.

★ It's OK to make mistakes.

★ Treating yourself with kind words and actions is the most effective way to avoid losing your shit again in the near future.

If you've got years of experience doing just the opposite, self-compassion is going to be a major mental shift. It's not going to come easily at first, and it's going to be extra tough to summon in the aftermath of a rough moment. So do the best you can, and remember this: *There is no reason to punish yourself for losing your shit with your kids.* It's not going to fix anything or make the situation any better. In fact, it's almost certainly going to trigger you even more, making it even more likely that you'll explode all over again. Self-compassion isn't about ignoring the issue or letting yourself off the hook, it's about noticing that you're struggling, reminding yourself that you're not alone, and treating yourself with kindness. It's about getting yourself into a better headspace so you can think clearly and make better choices going forward. So let's do that instead.

CURIOSITY
It's Not Just for the Kids

There's one other way to trick yourself into calming down, and it's a pretty cool one. Get curious about yourself, your triggers, and, yes, your loss of shit. Each time you do, you're turning on your adulting brain, treating yourself with compassion, and getting clear on what just went down and what you can do differently next time. It's pretty much the opposite of beating yourself up, getting all JADED, or shutting everything down. Think about the last time someone was interested in you, truly curious in whatever you were going through without rushing to judgment. It felt good, right? I'll bet you felt calmer, more connected, and more empowered to move forward. Fortunately, we can bring that same interested attitude to our own experience.

Curiosity is a powerful approach not only because it's inherently kind, but because it's our best shot at getting helpful, useful information about what actually happened. Your brain might automatically leap to old unhelpful stories about how awful and useless you are or what a punk your kid is, but now you know better. You're not going to take that bait. Instead, when you get curious and take a moment to investigate and notice what you're feeling, thinking, and experiencing, you're more likely to remember that you haven't slept in three days and your parents have been obsessively texting you

QUESTIONS TO ASK YOURSELF BEFORE, DURING, OR AFTER YOU LOSE YOUR SHIT

ONCE YOU'RE CALM enough to think clearly, here are some curiosity questions that might be useful:

★ What am I thinking? What am I feeling?

★ What is happening in my body? Am I exhausted? In pain? In need of food, water, or caffeine?

★ What is triggering me? What else is going on in my life?

★ Is the time of day or year relevant to my situation? Are there any major events coming up that might be stressing me out?

★ How can I calm myself down? What do I need right now? What can I put down or let go of, even for just a few minutes?

★ What do my kids need? Why are they pushing my buttons? Are they tired, hungry, or getting sick? Are they dealing with any major transitions or changes? Developmental milestones?

★ Who can I text or call for help or a break?

about their annual Ugly Sweater Holiday Party. Once you realize that, you can choose to silence your phone and get some sleep, either of which would be a more effective response than wallowing in your own self-pity.

But the awesomeness doesn't stop there. Curiosity is a great way to pull yourself out of a funk. Whenever your buttons get all lit up, each time you get stuck in a cranky, pissy, about-to-lose-your-shit headspace, get curious about, well, anything. If you're too wound up to think clearly about what you're feeling or doing, then do anything that will activate your curious brain. Read a riddle book, fit a piece into a puzzle, or sweep the floor. (Yes, sweeping is a curiosity exercise, especially when you live with kids. You have to inspect the floor pretty damn carefully unless you feel like sweeping three more times.) Even if you don't get any relevant information, you'll be cooling off your buttons. Just like compassion, curiosity is a function of your prefrontal cortex; whenever you can get curious about anything, you're powering up the very part of your brain that will help you not lose it again.

> **Curiosity is a great way to pull yourself out of a funk.**

Once you're calm enough to get curious about your body, feelings, and thoughts, do that. Were your shoulders tense? Were you fantasizing about running away? Solo trip to the beach, anyone? Or were you getting all twitchy and irritable, micromanaging every move your kid made? Whatever it is, try not to judge it or get frustrated with yourself. Just notice it and keep being curious. As you get more insight into what happens to you each time you explode, you'll get better at knowing what to look for, including the warning signs that will remind you to cool off the next time you're ready to blow.

The more you practice curiosity, the more easily it will come to you. Just do what you can to remember that the point here is to be nice to yourself. Don't mistake what I'm suggesting for some version of "WTF is wrong with me?" or "How the hell did I screw this up again?" This isn't an interrogation, so if you end up feeling like you're either the suspect with a spotlight blinding you or a bad cop getting all up in your own face, please go back and reread the compassion section and do that stuff instead.

Curiosity is a crucial first step, and for the best results, take yourself seriously. Don't blow yourself off. Don't realize you haven't peed in twelve hours and then not freaking pee. It's really hard to keep it together when you're worried about wetting your pants. If you notice that you're barreling through your days feeling lonely, stressed, or overwhelmed, talk to someone. Reach out for some support. And if you have a nagging sense that your freak-out might have something to do with your childhood or something else from your past, don't ignore it or pretend that it's not real, because whatever it is will keep triggering you until you deal with it.

Asking these questions can be incredibly hard and finding the answers can be even harder. Hell, even figuring out *which* questions to ask can be rough. It's OK to not know, and you don't have to figure it out alone. Reading about parenting and writing in a journal can help you wonder about and reflect on your experience. And remember that there are experts who can help you. Therapists, counselors, coaches, and clergy members are professionally curious, and when you find the right one, you'll feel calm and connected, rather than judged or interrogated.

Reconnecting
HOW TO MAKE NICE WITH YOUR KIDS

· ● · ● · ● ● · · · · · · ● ●

I promised that we would talk about reconnecting with your kids after the shitsplosion is over. Despite the fact that this book is about you and not about them, we're going to talk about them.

Checking in with your kiddo after a major meltdown is crucial. Toxic tantrums are discombobulating and confusing for everyone, and your kids get just as triggered as you do. However, their nervous systems are still developing, which means that chronic stress or frequent ruptures may have long-lasting detrimental effects. In addition, triggered kids are more likely to push buttons, which is not what you're going for, especially when you're working so hard to not lose your shit again.

Reconnecting with parents and other caregivers is a powerful and effective way to help children get calm and grounded. It can also help rebuild your relationship, which is important for lots of different reasons. Talking to your kids will help them understand what happened so they don't go making all sorts of inaccurate assumptions, like, say, that it was all their fault and they're terrible children.

There are a million ways to reconnect with your kid. An apology is a great place to start, and yes, you can absolutely positively 100 percent apologize to your child without undermining your own authority or upending the power dynamic in the family. Your apology will help strengthen your relationship, increase your child's respect for you, and as an added bonus, you'll be modeling the very behavior you want them to practice as well. That's good stuff right there.

In addition, apologizing for your behavior doesn't mean your kid wasn't being a turkey or pushing your buttons and it doesn't mean there won't be another conversation and maybe even some limit setting after the apology. But you need to set aside that issue for now. Your children won't be able to hear what you're saying or think clearly about what you're trying to teach them if their little brains and bodies are still flooded with stress hormones. So hold off on The Big Talk until everyone is cooled off again. There's an easy way to remember this: *connection before redirection*. So calm down, apologize to your child, and own your shit.

> Calm down, apologize to your child, and own your shit.

Here's how *not* to do this:

"I'm sorry if I yelled, but I freaking asked you a million times to stop throwing that damn ball in the house and you just didn't listen."

"I'm sorry I got mad, but you're being annoying and what the hell do you want from me?!"

Sticking the word *sorry* into a sentence doesn't automatically make it an apology. Both of those nonapologies are just more shit-losing in disguise, and you know it and I know it, and your kid sure as hell knows it even if they don't realize it. If that's what comes blasting out of your mouth, it's probably a good time for you to Notice, Pause, and Do Literally Anything Else. Once you're really calm, you can offer a meaningful apology, which generally has three parts:

1. Take responsibility for your behavior. Own your role in the situation, whatever it was.

2. Say you're sorry. Simple as that.

3. Make a plan for moving forward. Explain what you're going to do differently, and how it will help.

Here's an example of what it might sound like: "I'm sorry I yelled at you. I felt frustrated when you didn't put your shoes on. But yelling wasn't a good choice, and I apologize. Maybe we can try to help each other and be a team; you try hard to be a good listener and I'll try hard not to shout again. How does that sound?"

A few more notes on apologies:

★ **You can always identify or acknowledge your feelings, but you never have to apologize for how you feel.** You don't have to say you're sorry for feeling cranky or frustrated or exhausted or anything else. There is absolutely nothing wrong with any emotion, ever, no matter how yucky it may feel. You may, however, need to apologize for your behavior. The distinction between how you *feel* and what you *do* is an important one for both you and your children. The ability to experience difficult feelings without acting on them is a powerful life skill (and one that you probably need more practice with if you're reading this book).

★ **Don't make promises you can't keep.** Don't say you'll never lose it again, as that's unlikely to happen. (I mean, c'mon. I wrote this freaking book and I still lose it with my kids sometimes.) You should, however, make a plan for moving forward whenever possible. The predictability of knowing what will come next will help everyone feel even more grounded and calm. We're not going for a Life Plan here, we're just going for a Survive-Until-Bedtime Plan.

★ **Resist the urge to overtalk or overexplain.** Say what needs to be said as succinctly and clearly as you can. Too many words or explanations will cloud the moment and confuse your child. If you're not sure what I'm talking about, think about Miss Othmar, the teacher from the Peanuts comic. She speaks only in *wah-wah*'s, and that's all your kids will hear if you try to talk to them when they're still worked up. After the moment has passed, and everyone is chill again, you can find some time to talk about their role in what happened, if that's relevant.

★ **It's OK if apologizing is hard for you.** It's hard for a lot of folks, and it will get easier with practice. Chances are you'll have lots of opportunities to practice. If it's really hard for you, try *not* making eye contact while you do it. Sit next to your kiddo on the couch. Stand near them at the kitchen counter. Talk while you're in the car. Staying close to your child without staring at them or getting all up in their space will bring the intensity of the moment down a notch, which is often helpful.

★ **Notice if you're expecting a specific response from your child** (an apology, a hug, etc) and you start getting all twitchy when you don't get it. If that's the case, you're probably still triggered and at risk of blowing up again. Try to resist ranting about how it's their turn to apologize and they need to take responsibility for their actions and blah blah blah. This is just another version of losing your shit, and it's not helpful. Step away, take a few deep breaths, get yourself a glass of cold water, turn up the tunes, and give yourself a minute to calm down until you're ready to try again.

While reconnecting with your child may start with an apology, it doesn't have to end there. The extent to which you need to rebuild your relationship will depend on several factors, including the intensity and duration of your shit-loss, and how things have been going between you two recently. Have you been able to spend quality time together, or have you been unavailable, distracted, or stressed because of work, family, or financial issues, for example? The more distant you feel from your child, the more you need to work on managing your temper and being as present and patient as possible.

Reconnecting with your child after a tense moment can take many forms, but it's not about forcing them to spend time with you. Rather, it's about *attunement*, which means doing the best you can to get in sync with what's going on with your kiddo, and proceeding from there. You can draw from what you know about how your child copes and responds in times of stress; what has worked in the past and what hasn't. Do you have a sense of how they're feeling, what they might need, and how you can be a part of that? Some children crave a snuggle, others might want to play a game or read a book. A little time in the kitchen sharing a snack or shaking your tushies together can go a long way toward easing the tension for some children.

> While reconnecting with your child may start with an apology, it doesn't have to end there.

Other kids, however, may prefer time alone to draw, read, or play outside on their own. Your child may need some down time to relax and regroup, or they may still be angry or upset. Respect that need and give them space. Remember, at this moment, *it's not about you.* It's about paying attention to what your child needs and responding in kind.

The same goes for you; you also need to notice what you need and decide how and when (but not if!) to take care of yourself. It can feel like a tricky balancing act at times, but it will get easier with practice. For example, if you've been able to apologize but you're still triggered, do what you can to get the time and space you need. If you can't get any space (because, you know, kids), then you want to slooooow everything way down, hyper-focus on doing one thing at a time, and take lots and lots of deep breaths. This too shall pass.

If you can get some space, and your child is old enough to understand, tell them what's going on. Say something like, "I still feel tired and upset, and I don't want to yell again. I need some quiet time. Can I set you up with a book or toy while I rest?" You're not being rude or shirking your parenting duties; you're taking care of yourself so you can be a more effective parent going forward, and you're modeling exactly how you'd like your kids to respond the next time they're triggered.

The last step toward protecting and nurturing your relationship with your children is doing whatever it takes to reduce the likelihood that you will lose it again. While it's true that Rupture, Repair, Repeat is the cycle of parent-child relationships, too many toxic ruptures will weaken the connection and the trust between you two, no matter how hard you work at repair. After each explosion, make some time to reflect on what happened. Self-awareness is the crucial first step toward change. What triggered you? How have you been doing with your BuRPs recently? What changes do you need to make in the next day or two to manage or reduce your triggers and take care of yourself? What longer-term plans do you need to work toward? Be honest with yourself; accepting the reality of your challenges is necessary if you're going to take effective action.

This isn't a time to judge or berate yourself; that's counterproductive. Curiosity and self-compassion are your best moves here; They'll help you get the clarity and insight you need to move forward. Remember that you're not a bad parent; you've just been doing a really tough job without the right information, resources, and support. Fortunately, that's all about to change.

Congratulations! You made it to the end of a parenting book! If nothing else, please take that as further evidence that you are, in fact, a good parent, no matter how recently you lost your shit with your kids. We've covered a lot of information, from the neuroscience behind your meltdowns to my not-at-all patented yet highly powerful strategy of Notice, Pause, and Do Literally Anything Else. Hopefully, you're feeling inspired to make some changes around support, singletasking, or screen time, but if you're feeling overwhelmed about where to start, that's OK too. Change feels hard, especially when you haven't slept in six months. I get it, which is why I've summarized the book's key points, and offered suggestions that will help you get started. All you have to do is turn the page.

In the meantime, do your best to remember that parenting is hard for everyone, and you're definitely not alone in your shit-loss struggles. And try to treat yourself with the kindness and patience you hope to have for your kids. That's a great place to start.

Keep Your Shit Together

A Recap of Key Points and How to Put It All into Practice

W oo-hoo! You made it! You've read the whole book! Or you skipped to the end in hopes of getting the short version! Either way, great job. We've explored a lot here, so I've put together a quick reference you can return to without having to go through the entire book.

THE MOST IMPORTANT POINTS

1. When it comes to parenting, being awesome and screwing up are not mutually exclusive.

2. Parenting is incredibly hard. It's hard for all of us. If you're doing it without the right information, support, resources, and rest, you're going to lose your shit. This is not because you're a bad parent; it's because you're human.

3. You're always practicing something, whether it's something you want to get better at or not.

4. The goal here is progress, not perfection. Perfection can suck it.

5. We all have triggers. A trigger is anything that makes it more likely that you will lose your shit with your kids. It does this by making your buttons bigger, brighter, and more sensitive to being pushed.

6. While it is technically true that kids can be both triggers and button pushers, for the purposes of this book and your sanity, they're button pushers. Pushity push push push.

7. Identifying your triggers is the first step toward minimizing their impact. From that place of awareness, you can accept that your triggers are real and that they really light up your buttons. Awareness and acceptance lead to effective action.

8. The four nonnegotiable BuRPs (Button Reduction Practices) for cooling down your buttons are Single-Tasking, Sleep, Support, and Self-Compassion.

9. The following BurRPs will also help you stay calm in the face of chaos: Simplify, Stretch, Seek Silence, Slow Down, Say Thank You, and Breathe.

10. In addition to taking care of your buttons, you must also take space—physical and psychological—from your children. That's not bad parenting; just the opposite. You'll be more present and patient and less likely to freak out when you've had a little break.

11. The next time you're on the verge of losing it, or even mid-meltdown, all you need to do is Notice, Pause, and Do Literally Anything Else. Grab your oxygen mask and start breathing.

12. You always have another chance to get your shit together, even after you've lost it. Self-compassion and curiosity are powerful strategies for getting calm and reconnecting after an explosive moment.

13. This parenting gig is far too serious to be taken seriously. Try to laugh it off whenever you can.

MAKING IT HAPPEN

This would be a good time to grab a pen and paper so you can jot down any thoughts or ideas that come to mind as you go along; getting out of your cluttered mind will help you think more clearly. It will also make it more likely that you'll remember your triggers, BuRPs, and Literally Anything Elses in heated moments.

While the following suggestions roughly follow the order of the book, you don't have to practice them as they're written here. Do what you can when you can.

Notice and let go of any unhelpful "bad parent / bad kid" stories that are weighing you down. You may have to let go of these thoughts sixty times in sixty minutes, but that's better than drowning in them.

Make a list of your triggers. Review Chapter 3 (and if necessary consult the long list of potential triggers that starts on page 210), and think about what's going on in your life, in both big and small moments. Notice what's happening each time you lose it with your kids. Remember that triggers in other parts of your life can still light up your buttons and make them more sensitive to being pushed by your children.

Notice your tells. How do you know when your buttons are ablaze, just begging to be pushed? Does your face get hot? Your breathing get tight? Do your shoulders go up to your ears? Do you get irritable and snappy? Do you space out and fantasize about running away? Recognizing your tells is a powerful step toward calming yourself down.

Practice single-tasking as often as possible. Doing just one thing at a time will reduce your stress, as well as the likelihood that you'll lose your keys and your temper. Pick one or two activities that you do every day and generally enjoy (showering, drinking your coffee, reading to your kids, exercising, etc.) and make a point to stay as present as possible while you're doing it. In general, do whatever you can to get your mind and body in sync whenever you can, especially when you're with your children.

Make a plan for all of the shit you're going to do so you won't lose your shit. Sleep more? Hire a babysitter one night a week? Start a gratitude practice? Which practices will most effectively help you manage your triggers? What feels most feasible to tackle now? Remember that change takes time, and it's rarely easy. Cut yourself a whole lotta slack when you fall off the wagon; it will make it way easier to get back on.

Make a plan to get some space away from your children. Talk to your support system and parenting partner if you have one, and figure out what works for you. Remember, this is good for you, good for your kids, and really good for your relationship.

Repeat after me: Notice, Pause, and Do Literally Anything Else. Notice, Pause, and Do Literally Anything Else. Noticing that you are about to explode—or that you're mid-explosion, or that the freak-out has already happened and now you need to get calm so you can reconnect—is your superpower. It's the magic moment when you can pause, breathe, and get yourself just calm enough to Do Literally Anything Else.

Make a list of your Literally Anything Elses. Review Chapter 8 and write out whatever you think will work for you. Tape this list to your refrigerator, your mirror, and your child's forehead. Review it frequently.

Remember that you will still lose it, and that there are steps you can take after the shit has already hit the fan to reduce the likelihood that it will happen again soon. Self-compassion is key, so jot down a few phrases that you might say to a good friend who is struggling, and say these to yourself. Remind yourself that parenting is hard for everyone, and we all lose it sometimes.

You can also get curious about what's happening, for both you and your kids. What's going on? What are you thinking? Feeling? What do you need? What do they need? When was the last time you ate something? Slept through the night? Did something fun? What can you do now to take care of yourself and your kids (in that order)?

Reconnect with your child. Get yourself calm enough to apologize, and then do it. Remember: Rupture, repair, repeat, and connection before redirection.

And when all else fails, just remember that you don't have to be a perfect parent to be a great parent, and even the best of us lose our shit from time to time. Keep breathing. You got this.

A Ridiculously Long List of Potential Triggers

I n the event that you're having a hard time identifying your triggers, I've assembled an insanely long list for you to consider. Hopefully you will find this helpful and not stressful; if at any point you notice that you are freaking out, STOP READING. Put this book down, pet your cat, get some fresh air, and come back when you're in a better place to spend a little time considering what might be lighting up your buttons. That's the first step toward getting clear on how to calm yourself down, both in general and in response to challenging moments.

BASIC PERSONAL NEEDS

★ Hunger and/or hanger (the anger that comes from being too hungry)

★ Lack of regular exercise and movement

★ Not enough downtime, leisure time, or alone time

★ Sleep deprivation, fatigue, and exhaustion

★ Diet: too much junk food and other crap and not enough broccoli and brussels sprouts

SENSORY SENSITIVITIES
(They're not just for kids!)

★ Clutter in your living or workspace

★ Chaos, especially during transitions

★ Loud or sudden noises (which may or may not be coming from your children. Ahem)

★ Bright or flashing lights

★ Strong or unpleasant smells (which also may or may not be coming from your children)

★ Strong or unpleasant flavors or tastes

★ Too much or too frequent physical touch (See above re: your children)

★ Itchy, rough, restrictive, or otherwise uncomfortable clothing

★ Fast or erratic movement

★ Being in large crowds of people

★ Being in small spaces

★ Being too hot or too cold

★ Unpleasant or strong emotions, including anger, sadness, anxiety, frustration, boredom, regret, fear, grief, confusion, guilt, shame, resentment, joy, excitement, anticipation, and love

STRESS AND OVERWHELM

★ Attentional issues, including struggles with distraction and disorganization

★ Chronic stress, worry, and burnout

★ Constantly rushing or hurrying

★ An endless list of errands, tasks, and chores

★ Forgetting, losing, dropping, or breaking things

★ Lack of support in your personal, parental, and/or professional roles

★ Multitasking, especially when one of your tasks involves your children

★ Overscheduling and chronic busyness

★ Obsessively staring at and swiping through your smartphone

SOCIAL MEDIA STRESS

★ Seeing unexpected bad news

★ Being reminded of painful memories

★ Learning that you've been left out of or missed a community or social event

★ Doubting your parenting decisions or style as a result of other people's posts or advice

★ Being reminded of your own vulnerabilities at inopportune times (seeing a picture of a family's high-end vacation reminds you of your current financial stressors, for example)

★ Constant exposure to scary, confusing, or upsetting local or national news

★ Getting tangled up in misunderstood, unpleasant, or rude online conversations

★ Being harassed or bullied online

FAMILY AND RELATIONSHIP ISSUES

★ Family stress, which may include tense, abusive, or unresolved relationships with members of your immediate or extended family

★ Marriage or relationship stress, which can range from frequent bickering or verbal conflict to physical altercations and domestic violence

★ Visiting or spending time with challenging family members

★ Divorce, stepparenting, or living in a blended family

★ Living in the "sandwich" generation—caregiving for parents or other family members while you're also raising your own children

PARENTING CHALLENGES

Quick reminder from Chapter 3: While you can be triggered by your child, for the purposes of this book, we are thinking of your kids as button pushers, not triggers. Some aspects of the parenting experience may be particularly challenging for you, and that's normal. Your buttons are your buttons, which means it's your job to manage them.

★ Raising children with significant or ongoing physical, behavioral, developmental, attentional, or emotional challenges

★ Your child's age or developmental stage, especially if that age or stage was particularly hard for you as a child

★ Constant bickering or sibling rivalry

★ New experiences you couldn't anticipate and don't know how to manage

★ The stress of balancing work and parenting

★ The stress of staying home with your children full-time

★ Worry about whether or not your children are developing and behaving typically

★ Unmet expectations about your children's behavior and development

★ Pressure or judgment—real or perceived—from other parents or family members

★ Anxiety about how to parent correctly; lack of confidence in your parenting abilities

★ Activities or events that you would prefer not to attend but feel compelled to anyway

★ Holidays or vacations (which I prefer to think of as "trips with kids")

★ Snow days, sick days, or any other days that unexpectedly leave you home with your kids or scrambling for childcare

★ Single parenting, whether by choice or due to death, divorce, having a spouse in the military, or any other reason

★ Frequently losing your shit with your kids (Yep, this one can be both the result of being triggered and a fresh new trigger as well.)

LIFE-CYCLE MILESTONES FOR YOU AND YOUR FAMILY MEMBERS

Many life-cycle events can be painful, joyous, and overwhelming. It can be helpful to remember that even the happiest ones may trigger you, perhaps by bringing up difficult memories or unanticipated concerns about what may come next.

★ Pregnancy

★ Birth or adoption

★ Developmental changes (learning to walk, puberty, etc.)

★ Starting school, moving up through grades

★ Baptisms, christenings, or baby-naming ceremonies

★ Bar/bat mitzvahs, confirmations, sweet sixteens, or quinceañeras

★ Your kids getting their driver's licenses (EGAD!)

★ Graduations

★ Going to college

★ Getting a first job or changing jobs

★ Moving out of the house

★ Marriage

★ Retirement

★ Death

DAILY/MONTHLY/ YEARLY CYCLES

★ Time of day (early birds vs. night owls; the witching hour)

★ Anniversaries (milestones, weddings, losses)

★ Birthdays

★ Holidays (Christmas, Thanksgiving, Mother's Day, Father's Day, etc.)

★ Seasonal changes, including SAD (seasonal affective disorder)

★ Weather-related stressors

FINANCIAL STRESS AND RELATED CHALLENGES

★ Cash-flow problems

★ Debt

★ Insufficient income

★ Inconsistent or unreliable transportation

★ Insecure or inadequate housing

★ Lack of quality or affordable medical care for you and your family

★ Lack of quality or affordable childcare for your children

★ Spending beyond your means

JOB AND EMPLOYMENT STRESS

★ Unemployment or underemployment

★ Boring or uninteresting work

★ Inconvenient or inconsistent shift schedules

★ Lack of professional support

★ Major deadlines

★ Overwhelming responsibilities

★ Abusive supervisors or colleagues

★ Toxic workplaces

MENTAL HEALTH, MENTAL ILLNESS, AND ADDICTION IN YOU AND YOUR FAMILY

★ Alcohol or drug use, abuse, or addiction

★ Anxiety, panic disorder, or obsessive-compulsive disorder

★ Depression, bipolar disorder, or other major mental illnesses

★ Attention-deficit hyperactivity disorder (ADHD) or related executive-functioning disorders

★ A childhood marked by addiction, abuse, neglect, or underparenting

★ History of trauma and/or post-traumatic stress disorder

★ Internet, gaming, pornography, or gambling overuse or addiction

★ Self-harm or suicidal thoughts or feelings

PHYSICAL CHANGES AND CHALLENGES FOR YOU AND/OR YOUR FAMILY

★ Chronic pain and illnesses

★ Significant or life-changing diagnoses

★ Developmental or physical disabilities

★ Frequent trips to doctors, clinics, urgent care, or emergency departments

★ Miscarriages or infertility

★ Hormonal shifts, due to menstrual cycle, pregnancy, perimenopause, or menopause

★ Allergies that require frequent monitoring or awareness

★ Minor illnesses, infections, and injuries that result in kids staying home or parents missing work

★ Injuries of any sort

★ Colds, flus, and any number of insane viruses you've never heard of until your child went to day care for the first time

COMMUNITY AND ENVIRONMENTAL STRESS AND OPPRESSION

★ Exposure to systemic or individual racism, homophobia, misogyny, ableism, or any other forms of oppression in your home, work, or community environment

★ Living in an unsafe community or neighborhood

★ Anxiety and stress related to political or legal issues

CRISES AND TRAUMAS

★ Accidents and injuries

★ Incarcerations

★ Death or loss (including loss of a pet)

★ Mass shootings (WHY IS THIS STILL A THING?)

★ Natural disasters (earthquakes, fires, floods, storms)

★ Loss of childcare

★ Loss of job or employment

★ Loss of housing or moving residences

★ Unexpected diagnoses

Some Awesome Parenting Books That Will Also Help You Not Lose Your Shit

★ *The Good News About Bad Behavior: Why Kids Are Less Disciplined Than Ever—And What to Do About It* by Katherine Reynolds Lewis

★ *The Happy Kid Handbook: How to Raise Joyful Children in a Stressful World* by Katie Hurley

★ *How to Be a Happier Parent: Raising a Family, Having a Life, and Loving (Almost) Every Minute* by KJ Dell'Antonia

★ *Ignore It! How Selectively Looking the Other Way Can Decrease Behavioral Problems and Increase Parenting Satisfaction* by Catherine Pearlman, PhD, LCSW

★ *Strong as a Mother: How to Stay Healthy, Happy, and (Most Importantly) Sane from Pregnancy to Parenthood: The Only Guide to Taking Care of YOU!* by Kate Rope

★ *Parenting from the Inside Out: How a Deeper Self-Understanding Can Help You Raise Children Who Thrive* by Daniel J. Siegel, MD, and Mary Hartzell, MEd

★ *Simplicity Parenting: Using the Extraordinary Power of Less to Raise Calmer, Happier, and More Secure Kids* by Kim John Payne, MEd, and Lisa Ross

★ *The Tantrum Survival Guide: Tune In to Your Toddler's Mind (and Your Own) to Calm the Craziness and Make Family Fun Again* by Rebecca Schrag Hershberg, PhD

AND MY TWO PREVIOUS BOOKS:

★ *Parenting in the Present Moment: How to Stay Focused on What Really Matters*

★ *Ready, Set, Breathe: Practicing Mindfulness with Your Children for Fewer Meltdowns and a More Peaceful Family*